THE DANISH ART OF HAPPINESS

Embrace Hygge to Find Comfort and Joy
in Challenging Times

Freja Andersen

© Copyright 2023 - Freja Andersen - All rights reserved.

The following Book is reproduced below with the goal of providing information that is as accurate and reliable as possible. Regardless, purchasing this Book can be seen as consent to the fact that both the publisher and the author of this book are in no way experts on the topics discussed within and that any recommendations or suggestions that are made herein are for entertainment purposes only. Professionals should be consulted as needed prior to undertaking any of the action endorsed herein.

This declaration is deemed fair and valid by both the American Bar Association and the Committee of Publishers Association and is legally binding throughout the United States.

Furthermore, the transmission, duplication, or reproduction of any of the following work including specific information will be considered an illegal act irrespective of if it is done electronically or in print. This extends to creating a secondary or tertiary copy of the work or a recorded copy and is only allowed with the express written consent from the Publisher. All additional right reserved.

The information in the following pages is broadly considered a truthful and accurate account of facts and as such, any inattention, use, or misuse of the information in question by the reader will render any resulting actions solely under their purview. There are no scenarios in which the publisher or the original author of this work can be in any fashion deemed liable for any hardship or damages that may befall them after undertaking information described herein.

Additionally, the information in the following pages is intended only for informational purposes and should thus be thought of as universal. As befitting its nature, it is presented without assurance regarding its prolonged validity or interim quality. Trademarks that are mentioned are done without written consent and can in no way be considered an endorsement from the trademark holder.

Table of Content

Introduction
9

Chapter 1: The Philosophy of Hygge
13

Origins and Cultural Significance of Hygge
13

Understanding the Core Principles and Values of Hygge
17

How Hygge Aligns with the Human Desire for Comfort and Contentment
23

Chapter 2: Creating a Cozy Home Environment
29

How to Transform Living Spaces Into Cozy and Inviting Sanctuaries
29

The Role of Lighting, Natural Elements, and Soft Textures in Creating a Hygge Atmosphere.
33

Tips for Decluttering and Organizing Spaces to Enhance a Sense of Comfort and Well-Being
39

Chapter 3: Hygge in Relationships and Social Interactions
51

How Hygge Can Strengthen Connections and Foster Intimacy
51

The Importance of Meaningful Conversations, Quality Time, and Shared Experiences
57

Suggestions for Incorporating Hygge into Gatherings, Celebrations, and Everyday Interactions with Loved Ones
61

Chapter 4: Embracing Hygge in Self-Care and Mindfulness
67

The Role of Hygge in Self-Care Practices and Nurturing One's Well-Being
67

Mindfulness Techniques and How They Relate to Hygge
73

Suggestions and Ideas for Incorporating Hygge into Relaxation Rituals, Self-Reflection, and Embracing Solitude
78

Chapter 5: Hygge Across Seasons and Celebrations
85

How Hygge Can Be Adapted to Different Seasons and Festivities
85

Hygge Practices During Winter, Spring, Summer, and Autumn.

93

The Hygge Traditions Associated with Specific Holidays and Celebrations
105

Chapter 6: Hygge Beyond Denmark: Similar Concepts in Different Cultures
121

Cozy and Contentment-Focused Concepts in Other Cultures
121

Danish "Hygge", Swedish "Mys", or Norwegian "Kos": Difference and Similarities
125

Universal Human Desires: Comfort, Well-Being, and a Sense of Belonging
131

Conclusion
135

Embrace Hygge in Your Life
135

Prioritize Coziness, Mindfulness, and Togetherness for Overall Well-Being
138

Farewell...
140

Introduction

Welcome to the world of hygge! I am thrilled to have you join me on this journey of discovering the profound significance of hygge in improving our well-being, especially during challenging times. In this book, we will dive into the concept of hygge, exploring its essence and how it can bring comfort, joy, and a fresh perspective to our lives.

Have you ever longed for a feeling of warmth, contentment, and a sense of belonging? That's precisely what hygge (pronounced "hoo-ga") is all about. While it originated in Denmark, its embrace has spread far and wide, as people from all walks of life seek solace and a renewed sense of happiness.

Picture this: cozy evenings by the fire, surrounded by loved ones, wrapped in a soft blanket. Or imagine the sheer delight of sipping a hot cup of tea while watching the raindrops dance on your windowpane. These are the moments that hygge encapsulates—the feeling of being present and finding joy in life's simple pleasures.

In our fast-paced world, where stress seems to be ever-present, hygge beckons us to slow down and create pockets of tranquility. It urges us to cultivate inviting spaces that envelop us in comfort and provide a refuge from the chaos of everyday life. These cozy environments have the power to soothe our minds, relax our bodies, and nurture a sense of security.

But hygge goes beyond our physical surroundings. It shines a light on the importance of togetherness and the power of genuine connections. In a world that often feels disconnected and isolating, hygge encourages us to gather with loved ones, to engage in heartfelt conversations, and to create shared experiences. Through these connections, we find a sense of belonging, support, and emotional fulfillment.

Hygge also invites us to be mindful and fully present in the moment. It urges us to disconnect from technology, take a deep breath, and appreciate the beauty in the ordinary. By practicing mindfulness, we cultivate a heightened awareness of our surroundings, our emotions, and the present moment. This newfound mindfulness allows us to uncover joy and gratitude in the small details that often go unnoticed.

Throughout this book, we will embark on a journey together, exploring the principles and practices of hygge. I will share practical tips, inspiring stories, and reflective exercises to help you infuse hygge into your daily life. Whether you're going through a difficult time, seeking a sense of calm, or simply yearning for a more joyful existence, hygge has the potential to transform your well-being.

Before delving into the enchanting world of hygge and its transformative power, let us take a moment to reflect on the concept of happiness itself. Happiness is a deeply personal and subjective experience, unique to each and every one of us. It is not a destination to be reached, but rather a journey we embark upon, weaving through the tapestry of our lives. For some, happiness may be found in the warmth of human connections, in moments of laughter and shared experiences. For others, it may reside in solitude and self-reflection, finding peace in the quiet moments of introspection. Happiness can be found in the simplest of pleasures, in the embrace of a loved one, or in the gentle touch of nature. It is a mosaic of emotions, desires, and aspirations that create a sense of contentment and fulfillment. So, as we explore the realms of hygge, let us remember that happiness is a deeply personal quest, and that hygge serves as a guiding light, illuminating the path towards a more joyful and harmonious existence.

In this journey towards happiness, we discover that hygge serves as a cherished companion along the way. It beckons us to embrace the beauty of simplicity, to find solace in the cozy corners of our lives, and to savor the moments that ignite a spark of joy within us. Hygge invites us to cultivate a mindful awareness of the present, to immerse ourselves fully in the warmth and comfort of the here and now. It reminds us to nurture our relationships, to create spaces that radiate with tranquility, and to indulge in the little pleasures that bring us immense happiness. Hygge is not a fleeting indulgence but a way of life that transcends seasons and circumstances. It is a gentle reminder to seek out the small moments of bliss that exist in the everyday, for it is in these moments that we weave the tapestry of a truly fulfilling and hyggelig life. So, as we embark on this exploration of hygge, may we discover new depths of happiness, well-being, and all the exquisite wonders that come with embracing the art of cozy living.

So, my friend, grab your coziest blanket, light a candle, and get ready to immerse yourself in the warmth, the coziness, and the magic of hygge. Together, we will discover the comfort, connection, and profound beauty that lie within the embrace of hygge. Are you ready to embark on this transformative journey of happiness, self-discovery and well-being? Let's begin.

Chapter 1: The Philosophy of Hygge

Origins and Cultural Significance of Hygge

Hygge, a concept deeply rooted in Danish culture, carries a fascinating history and remarkable cultural significance. Originating from the challenging conditions of Denmark's long, dark winters, hygge emerged as a way for Danes to find comfort, warmth, and a sense of well-being. The term itself is believed to have its roots in Old Norse, where it referred to the feeling of security and protection. Over time, hygge evolved to encompass a broader meaning, encompassing coziness, intimacy, and a mindful appreciation of life's simple pleasures.

In Danish society, hygge is more than just a word – it is a way of life. It embodies the Danish ethos of fostering a sense of togetherness and prioritizing meaningful connections with family, friends, and community. Danes often create hyggelige (hygge-like) environments, characterized by soft lighting, comfortable furnishings, and cherished personal items. Candles, a quintessential element of hygge, cast a warm and soothing glow, enhancing the cozy ambiance.

The cultural significance of hygge extends beyond the physical environment. It reflects the Danish values of equality and inclusivity, as hygge can be experienced by anyone, regardless of their background or socioeconomic status. In fact, Denmark consistently ranks among the happiest countries in the world, and hygge is often cited as a contributing factor to their overall well-being. Hygge provides a refuge from the stresses of daily life, encouraging Danes to slow down, savor the present moment, and foster genuine connections with loved ones.

Hygge extends beyond the home and permeates various aspects of Danish culture. It is integrated into social gatherings, where friends and family come together for cozy meals, engaging conversations, and shared experiences. In workplaces, hygge is embraced through practices such as creating comfortable common areas, promoting work-life balance, and encouraging supportive relationships among colleagues.

The history of hygge dates back several centuries, with its roots embedded in Danish culture and traditions. The word "hygge" itself can be traced back to the 18th century, but the concept it represents has deeper historical origins. The origins of hygge can be attributed to the harsh Scandinavian winters, where long nights and bitter cold created a need for warmth, comfort, and togetherness. In the past, Denmark was primarily an agricultural society, and the winter months posed challenges for farmers and villagers alike. To cope with the darkness and isolation, Danes developed the concept of hygge as a way to find solace and create a sense of well-being.

Hygge evolved from the Old Norse word "hugr," which meant "mind" or "soul," and later took on the meaning of "security" or "protection." Over time, it encompassed a broader sense of creating a cozy atmosphere and fostering a feeling of contentment. Hygge became a way to combat the harsh realities of winter and prioritize the joys of companionship, warmth, and simple pleasures.

Throughout Danish history, hygge has been interwoven into everyday life. It is evident in the traditions of gathering around a crackling fireplace, sharing meals with loved ones, and finding joy in the company of friends and family. Hygge has influenced Danish architecture, interior design, and even city planning, with an emphasis on creating inviting and cozy spaces.

While hygge has always been a part of Danish culture, it gained wider recognition outside of Denmark in recent years. The concept has resonated with people around the world who seek respite from the fast-paced, digitally-driven modern lifestyle. Hygge has become synonymous with self-care, mindfulness, and finding happiness in life's simple pleasures.

By embracing hygge in our own lives, we can tap into the universal human desires for comfort, well-being, and a sense of belonging. It reminds us to slow down, appreciate the present moment, and foster connections with loved ones. Whether we find hygge in the cozy corners of our homes, in the warmth of shared meals, or in the simple joys of everyday life, it offers a pathway to greater contentment and a deeper appreciation for the little moments that bring us happiness. So let us open our hearts and embrace the art of hygge, allowing its gentle embrace to guide us towards a life filled with coziness, mindfulness, and togetherness.

Today, the history of hygge continues to unfold as it adapts and evolves in different cultures and contexts. It has become a global phenomenon, inspiring books, articles, and social media trends that celebrate the pursuit of coziness, relaxation, and meaningful connections.

By understanding the history of hygge, we gain a deeper appreciation for its cultural significance and its ability to bring comfort, well-being, and a sense of belonging not only to the Danish people but to people around the world seeking a more balanced and fulfilling way of life.

Understanding the Core Principles and Values of Hygge

In the realm of hygge, there exists a set of principles and values that guide the Danish way of life and infuse it with warmth, contentment, and a deep sense of well-being. These principles serve as the foundation for embracing hygge in our daily lives, allowing us to create an atmosphere of coziness, foster meaningful connections, and find joy in the simplest of pleasures. By understanding and embodying these hygge principles, we can cultivate a life that is centered around comfort, mindfulness, and togetherness. So, let us delve into the world of hygge principles and values, and discover how they can transform our perspective and enhance our overall sense of happiness and fulfillment.

Let's explore the core principles and values of hygge in more detail:

Coziness

Coziness lies at the heart of hygge. It encompasses creating a warm, inviting, and comfortable atmosphere. This can be achieved through soft lighting, candles, blankets, and cozy furnishings. Coziness extends beyond physical surroundings to encompass emotional comfort and a sense of security. It encourages us to slow down, relax, and indulge in life's simple pleasures.

Togetherness

Hygge places great emphasis on the value of meaningful connections and fostering a sense of togetherness. It encourages us to gather with loved ones, friends, and community members to share in joyful experiences. Whether it's cozying up with family around a fireplace or enjoying a meal with friends, the act of connecting and nurturing relationships is an essential aspect of hygge.

Mindfulness

Hygge encourages us to be present in the moment and cultivate mindfulness. It is about savoring and fully experiencing the here and now. By embracing mindfulness, we become more attuned to our surroundings, appreciating the beauty of small details and finding gratitude in everyday moments. Being mindful allows us to find joy and contentment in simple pleasures, fostering a deeper sense of well-being.

Simplicity

Hygge celebrates the beauty of simplicity and the joy found in life's uncomplicated moments. It prompts us to declutter our lives, both physically and mentally, and focus on what truly matters. By simplifying our surroundings, we create space for tranquility and allow ourselves to fully enjoy the present. Embracing simplicity helps reduce stress and cultivates a greater appreciation for the things that bring us happiness.

Gratitude

Hygge encourages a mindset of gratitude, recognizing and appreciating the blessings in our lives. It prompts us to focus on what we have rather than what we lack. By expressing gratitude for the cozy moments, the company of loved ones, and the little joys, we cultivate a positive outlook and a greater sense of contentment.

These core principles and values of hygge intertwine to create a holistic approach to well-being. By embracing coziness, togetherness, mindfulness, simplicity, and gratitude, we can create a harmonious and fulfilling life that prioritizes comfort, connection, and a deep appreciation for the present moment.

As we proceed on our journey, it's beneficial to familiarize ourselves with some additional insights on the core principles of hygge. These insights will continue to be encountered throughout our exploration, and understanding them will enhance our understanding and appreciation of hygge. They include:

Balance

Hygge promotes a balanced approach to life. It encourages finding a harmonious blend of relaxation and productivity, solitude and socializing, and indulgence and healthy habits. It reminds us to create a balance that nourishes our well-being and brings joy to our everyday lives.

Presence

Hygge emphasizes the importance of being fully present in the moment. It encourages us to put aside distractions, such as phones and screens, and engage in genuine connections and experiences. By being present, we can deepen our relationships, fully appreciate our surroundings, and find contentment in the here and now.

Self-Care

Hygge places a strong emphasis on self-care and nurturing oneself. It encourages us to prioritize our well-being by engaging in activities that bring us comfort, relaxation, and rejuvenation. This can include practicing self-care rituals like taking soothing baths, reading a book, enjoying a hot beverage, or spending time in nature.

Authenticity

Hygge celebrates authenticity and embracing one's true self. It encourages us to create environments and experiences that reflect our personal preferences, values, and interests. By being true to ourselves, we can foster a greater sense of comfort, belonging, and fulfillment.

Flexibility

While hygge is often associated with cozy indoor settings, it also acknowledges the importance of adaptability. Hygge can be experienced in various contexts, whether it's enjoying a picnic in nature, exploring a new city, or engaging in outdoor activities. It reminds us to be open to different experiences and to create hygge wherever we are.

Remember that hygge is a flexible concept that can be interpreted and applied in diverse ways. It's about finding what brings you comfort, joy, and a sense of well-being in your own life. By embracing these core principles, you can create your own hygge moments and cultivate a greater sense of happiness and fulfillment.

How Hygge Aligns with the Human Desire for Comfort and Contentment

Hygge speaks directly to our inherent longing for comfort and contentment. It understands our need for physical and emotional coziness, creating spaces and experiences that envelop us in a warm embrace. By surrounding ourselves with soft blankets, gentle lighting, and comfortable settings, we tap into our desire for comfort. Hygge also embraces simplicity, inviting us to find contentment in life's simple pleasures and appreciate the beauty of ordinary moments. It encourages mindfulness, allowing us to be fully present and savor the sensations that bring us joy. Hygge acknowledges our deep-seated need for connection and togetherness, prompting us to gather with loved ones and foster meaningful relationships. Additionally, it emphasizes self-care as a vital aspect of our well-being, reminding us to prioritize our own needs and find moments of rejuvenation. By embracing these aspects of hygge, we create a pathway to experiencing greater comfort, contentment, and a deeper sense of fulfillment in our lives.

Let's explore how hygge aligns with the human desire for comfort and contentment through an examination:

1. *Comfort:* Hygge resonates with our innate desire for comfort. It acknowledges the human need for physical and emotional coziness, creating environments and experiences that provide a sense of ease, warmth, and relaxation. By surrounding ourselves with soft blankets, gentle lighting, and comfortable furnishings, we create a space that nurtures our well-being and promotes a deep sense of comfort.

2. *Simplicity:* Hygge embraces simplicity, which aligns with our desire for contentment. In our fast-paced and often complex lives, we yearn for moments of simplicity and ease. By stripping away unnecessary distractions and focusing on the essentials, hygge helps us find contentment in life's simple pleasures. It reminds us to appreciate the beauty in ordinary moments and to

cultivate gratitude for the small joys that bring us comfort.

3. *Mindfulness:* Hygge aligns with our desire for contentment through mindfulness. By encouraging us to be fully present in the moment, hygge enables us to fully appreciate and immerse ourselves in the experiences that bring us comfort. Mindfulness allows us to savor the sensations, connections, and pleasures that enhance our well-being. It helps us let go of worries about the past or future and find contentment in the present.

4. *Connection:* Hygge acknowledges our innate desire for connection and community. Human beings are social creatures who seek companionship and meaningful relationships. Hygge fosters togetherness by encouraging us to gather with loved ones, share meals, engage in heartfelt conversations, and create cherished memories. These connections and shared experiences contribute to our overall sense of comfort, contentment, and belonging.

5. *Self-Care:* Hygge recognizes the importance of self-care in our pursuit of comfort and contentment. Taking care of ourselves physically, emotionally, and mentally is crucial for our well-being. Hygge encourages us to

prioritize self-care rituals, such as indulging in a warm bath, practicing relaxation techniques, or engaging in activities that bring us joy and replenish our energy. By tending to our own needs and finding moments of self-nurturing, we cultivate a sense of comfort and contentment within ourselves.

6. *Nature:* Hygge often incorporates a connection to nature, recognizing the calming and soothing effects it has on our well-being. Integrating natural elements like plants, fresh air, and natural materials into our surroundings can enhance the sense of comfort and contentment. Spending time in nature, whether it's a peaceful walk in the woods or enjoying a picnic in a park, can also be an integral part of the hygge experience.

7. *Rituals and Traditions:* Hygge embraces the significance of rituals and traditions in cultivating comfort and contentment. Engaging in repetitive activities or establishing comforting routines can provide a sense of stability and create a framework for relaxation. Whether it's brewing a cup of tea in the morning or engaging in a bedtime ritual, incorporating these practices into our lives adds a layer of comfort and familiarity.

8. *Food and Drink:* Hygge places importance on nourishing the body and soul through comforting food and drink. Enjoying hearty meals, indulging in homemade treats, and sipping warm beverages like hot chocolate or spiced tea can evoke feelings of coziness and contentment. Sharing these meals with loved ones further enhances the sense of togetherness and creates cherished moments of connection.

9. *Embracing Imperfections:* Hygge encourages us to embrace imperfections and find beauty in simplicity. It reminds us that perfection is not necessary for experiencing comfort and contentment. Instead, it celebrates the charm of handmade items, worn-in furniture, and imperfect moments. By letting go of unrealistic expectations, we create space for genuine joy and appreciate the authenticity of life's imperfections.

10. *Seasonal Awareness:* Hygge is attuned to the changing seasons and embraces the unique comforts they bring. It encourages us to adapt our surroundings and activities to suit the season. For example, cozying up by the fireplace during winter, enjoying outdoor picnics during spring, or basking in the warmth of the sun during summer. Being mindful of the seasons and embracing the specific pleasures they offer adds depth to our hygge experiences.

Overall, hygge aligns with our fundamental desire for comfort and contentment by embracing the elements of physical and emotional coziness, simplicity, mindfulness, connection, and self-care. It acknowledges the importance of creating spaces, experiences, and moments that cater to our well-being, allowing us to find comfort, contentment, and a deeper sense of fulfillment in our lives.

Chapter 2: Creating a Cozy Home Environment

How to Transform Living Spaces Into Cozy and Inviting Sanctuaries

Welcome to the transformative world of hygge, where we embark on a journey to create cozy and inviting sanctuaries within our living spaces.

In this modern age, our homes have become more than just living quarters - they are our personal retreats, places of comfort and solace. By following the principles of hygge, we can infuse our living spaces with warmth, relaxation, and a sense of well-being. In this list, we will explore practical steps to help you curate a haven that envelops you in comfort, invites you to unwind, and fosters a deep connection with yourself and those around you. Let's delve into the art of transforming your living spaces into cozy and inviting sanctuaries, where you can truly experience the joy and tranquility that hygge brings.

Here are some key steps to transform your living spaces into cozy and inviting sanctuaries following the principles of hygge:

Soften the Lighting

Create a warm and inviting atmosphere by incorporating soft, warm lighting. Use lamps with soft, dimmable bulbs instead of harsh overhead lighting. Add candles or string lights to create a cozy glow. Lighting plays a crucial role in setting the mood and ambiance, allowing you to relax and unwind.

Layer Textures and Fabrics

Embrace cozy textures and fabrics that invite you to touch and snuggle. Add plush rugs, soft blankets, and comfortable cushions to create a tactile and inviting environment. Mix and match different textures, such as wool, faux fur, or knitted fabrics, to add depth and warmth to your space.

Create Cozy Nooks

Designate specific areas in your living space as cozy nooks where you can retreat and unwind. Arrange a comfortable armchair or a window seat with soft cushions and blankets. Add a side table with a warm beverage or a stack of your favorite books. These cozy corners offer a sense of comfort and solitude, allowing you to relax and recharge.

Bring Nature Indoors

Incorporate elements of nature to create a connection with the outdoors. Place potted plants or fresh flowers in your living space to bring life and freshness. Natural elements not only add visual appeal but also contribute to a sense of tranquility and well-being.

Declutter and Simplify

Remove unnecessary clutter and create a sense of simplicity in your living space. Clutter can create visual and mental stress, so opt for minimalistic decor that promotes a calm and serene environment. Keep only the items that bring you joy and serve a purpose, allowing your space to feel open, organized, and inviting.

Foster Intimate Gatherings

Arrange your furniture in a way that encourages conversation and connection. Create an intimate seating arrangement that brings people closer together. Place cozy throws and pillows on the sofa to encourage relaxation and encourage interaction. The goal is to foster meaningful connections and togetherness within your living space.

Incorporate Scent and Sound

Engage your senses by incorporating pleasant scents and soothing sounds. Use scented candles, essential oil diffusers, or natural room sprays to fill your space with calming aromas. Play soft music or nature sounds to create a soothing background ambiance. These sensory elements can enhance the cozy and inviting atmosphere of your sanctuary.

Remember, the key to transforming your living spaces into cozy and inviting sanctuaries is to personalize them according to your preferences and needs. Let your creativity and individuality shine through as you apply these principles of hygge, creating a space that truly feels like a haven of comfort and well-being. Let's get a little deeper into this matter.

The Role of Lighting, Natural Elements, and Soft Textures in Creating a Hygge Atmosphere.

Imagine stepping into a living space that instantly wraps you in a warm embrace, a sanctuary where you can retreat from the outside world and find solace. The secret lies in the art of creating a hygge atmosphere, where the interplay of lights, textures, and natural elements brings forth a sense of comfort and contentment. Soft, warm lighting casts a gentle glow, guiding you into a realm of tranquility. Natural elements, from lush green plants to earthy materials, connect you to the soothing rhythms of nature, grounding you in the present moment. As you sink into plush cushions and wrap yourself in cozy blankets, the textures envelop you, inviting relaxation and rejuvenation. By thoughtfully incorporating these elements, you can transform your living space into a haven that engages the senses, evokes a deep sense of well-being, and embraces the essence of hygge. Let's explore the role of lighting, textures, and natural elements in crafting a sanctuary where comfort and contentment abound.

Lighting: Lighting plays a vital role in setting the mood and ambiance of a space, and it is a key element in creating a hygge atmosphere. Soft, warm lighting is preferred over harsh, bright lights. By using lamps with warm-toned bulbs, candles, or string lights, you can create a cozy and inviting glow that instantly transforms the atmosphere. The gentle flickering of candlelight and the warm hue of soft bulbs create a sense of relaxation and comfort. Dimmable lighting options allow you to adjust the brightness to your desired level, enhancing the cozy ambiance.

Integrate Natural Light: Make the most of natural light by allowing it to flow into your space. Keep windows unobstructed and use sheer or light curtains that allow sunlight to filter through. Natural light not only brightens your space but also boosts mood and promotes a connection to the outside world.

Introduce Nature-Inspired Elements: Bringing natural elements into your living space is another important aspect of creating a hygge atmosphere. Nature has a soothing and grounding effect on our well-being. Incorporate elements such as potted plants, fresh flowers, or a small indoor herb garden. Not only do they add visual appeal and a touch of greenery, but they also contribute to a sense of tranquility and connection with the outdoors. Nature-inspired decor, such as wooden furniture, stone accents, or woven baskets, can also infuse a space with a warm and earthy aesthetic.

Soften the Ambiance with Textiles: Soft textures play a significant role in creating a tactile and cozy environment. Embrace soft and plush materials that invite touch and comfort. Layer your living space with cozy blankets, fluffy cushions, and rugs with a luxurious feel. Opt for fabrics such as faux fur, knitted blankets, or velvet upholstery to add depth and warmth to your surroundings. The presence of these soft textures encourages relaxation, creating a cozy nook where you can unwind and find comfort.

Together, lighting, natural elements, and soft textures work harmoniously to create a hygge atmosphere that nurtures a sense of well-being and comfort. The warm and gentle lighting sets the ambiance, while the presence of natural elements connects us to the calming influence of the outdoors. Soft textures invite us to relax and indulge in the cozy embrace of our surroundings. By combining these elements, you can transform your living space into a haven that evokes feelings of contentment, relaxation, and a deep connection with the present moment.

However, there are other elements that you can take into consideration for an even better outcome.

Scent: The sense of smell plays a powerful role in creating a cozy ambiance. Consider incorporating pleasant scents into your living space. Choose scented candles, essential oil diffusers, or natural room sprays with calming fragrances like lavender, vanilla, or cinnamon. These aromas can evoke a sense of comfort and relaxation, further enhancing the hygge atmosphere.

Personal Touches: Adding personal touches to your living space can make it feel truly inviting and unique. Display cherished photographs, artwork, or sentimental items that evoke positive emotions and memories. Surround yourself with objects that hold special meaning or bring you joy. By infusing your personality into the space, it becomes a reflection of who you are, fostering a deeper sense of connection and comfort.

Mindful Arrangement: Pay attention to the arrangement of furniture and decor in your living space. Aim for a layout that promotes a sense of coziness and encourages intimate gatherings. Arrange seating areas to facilitate conversation and closeness. Create cozy nooks or reading corners that invite you to relax and unwind. Thoughtful and intentional placement of items can contribute to a harmonious and inviting atmosphere.

Engage the Senses: Consider engaging all the senses to enhance the hygge experience. Play soft, soothing music or nature sounds in the background to create a calming ambiance. Indulge in warm beverages like herbal tea or hot cocoa, allowing their comforting flavors to soothe your palate. Embrace the tactile experience of wrapping yourself in a soft blanket or sinking into a plush chair. By engaging multiple senses, you create a multi-dimensional and immersive hygge atmosphere.

Seasonal Adaptation: Embrace the changing seasons and adapt your living space accordingly. Integrate seasonal elements into your decor, such as autumn leaves, winter garlands, or spring blooms. Swap out cozy blankets and cushions to match the colors and textures of each season. By aligning your living space with the rhythms of nature, you can enhance the hygge experience and feel more connected to the world around you.

Choose Earthy and Neutral Tones: Opt for a color palette that reflects the hygge philosophy, focusing on earthy and neutral tones. Shades of beige, gray, warm browns, and muted pastels create a calming and harmonious atmosphere. These colors have a soothing effect and contribute to a sense of serenity and relaxation.

Cultivate a Sense of Hygge in Every Room: Extend the hygge philosophy beyond your living areas and infuse it into every room of your home. Create a cozy bedroom with soft bedding, dimmable lighting, and a clutter-free environment that promotes restful sleep. Transform your bathroom into a spa-like retreat with candles, natural scents, and plush towels. Embrace hygge even in your kitchen by surrounding yourself with warm and inviting elements like a cozy breakfast nook or a shelf with comforting ingredients and cookbooks.

Prioritize Mindful Activities: Create spaces within your home dedicated to mindful activities that promote relaxation and self-care. Designate a cozy reading corner with a comfortable chair and a small bookshelf. Set up a meditation or yoga area with soft lighting, cushions, and calming scents. By creating dedicated spaces for mindfulness, you encourage a deeper connection with yourself and a greater sense of well-being.

By implementing these additional tips and suggestions, you can further enhance the comfort, tranquility, and overall hygge experience in your living space. Remember, the key is to create an environment that nourishes your well-being, fosters connection, and allows you to fully embrace the joy of hygge in your everyday life.

Tips for Decluttering and Organizing Spaces to Enhance a Sense of Comfort and Well-Being

Step into the enchanting realm of decluttering and organizing, where the harmonious blend of simplicity and serenity transports you to a hygge-inspired oasis in your daily existence. In the fast-paced modern world, our living spaces often become a reflection of the chaos and busyness we encounter. However, by embracing the principles of hygge and adopting a mindful approach to decluttering and organizing, we can reclaim our spaces as sanctuaries of comfort, contentment, and tranquility. As we embark on this journey together, we will explore how the art of decluttering not only clears physical clutter but also frees our minds and hearts, allowing us to fully embrace the warmth and joy that hygge brings. So, let us embark on this voyage of transformation, where order and coziness blend harmoniously to create a space that nourishes the soul and invites us to savor life's simple pleasures.

Decluttering plays a crucial role in embracing the essence of hygge and creating a cozy and harmonious environment. Here's why decluttering is so important for hygge.

Clutter fills our physical space with distractions and visual noise, making it challenging to find a sense of peace and tranquility. By decluttering, we create space for serenity to bloom, allowing our surroundings to become a soothing refuge where we can unwind and recharge.

Hygge celebrates simplicity and the beauty found in the uncluttered. Decluttering helps us let go of excess possessions, freeing ourselves from the burden of material clutter. This act of simplifying allows us to focus on what truly matters, fostering a deeper connection with the things and experiences that bring us joy.

Decluttering requires us to engage in a process of mindful awareness. As we assess our belongings, we become attuned to what truly resonates with our hearts and aligns with our hygge lifestyle. This mindful evaluation helps us cultivate a deeper sense of gratitude and appreciation for the items we choose to keep, creating a more meaningful and intentional environment.

Our external environment has a profound impact on our internal well-being. Cluttered spaces can evoke feelings of stress, overwhelm, and unease. By decluttering, we create a calming and harmonious atmosphere that supports emotional well-being. It allows us to experience a sense of clarity, fostering a positive mindset and enabling us to fully embrace the cozy moments of hygge.

Hygge thrives in spaces that exude warmth and comfort. Decluttering creates room for cozy elements, such as soft blankets, plush cushions, and flickering candlelight, to take center stage. These cozy elements transform our spaces into inviting sanctuaries, enveloping us in a nurturing embrace and amplifying the hygge experience.

An uncluttered space promotes a smoother flow of energy and enhances the ease with which we navigate our surroundings. By removing physical barriers and distractions, we create an environment that supports relaxation, connection, and unhurried moments of hygge. It allows us to move through our spaces with grace and mindfulness, fostering a sense of calm and balance.

By embracing the practice of decluttering, we invite hygge into our lives on a deeper level. It paves the way for coziness, simplicity, and intentional living, transforming our spaces into havens of comfort and joy. As we release the unnecessary and create room for what truly matters, we embark on a journey of self-discovery and appreciation, savoring the moments of hygge that await us in our uncluttered and lovingly curated surroundings.

Here are some tips for decluttering and organizing spaces to enhance a sense of comfort and well-being in line with the hygge philosophy:

- _Embrace Minimalism:_ Hygge celebrates simplicity and embraces a clutter-free environment. Start by decluttering your space and removing items that no longer serve a purpose or bring you joy. Adopt a minimalist approach by keeping only the essentials and meaningful possessions. Remember, a clean and organized space creates a sense of calm and allows room for the cozy elements of hygge to shine.

- _Create Storage Solutions:_ Invest in practical storage solutions to keep your belongings organized and out of sight. Utilize baskets, bins, and storage boxes to neatly store items like blankets, books, or other essentials. Having designated places for everything not only reduces visual clutter but also makes it easier to find and enjoy the items you truly cherish.

- *Prioritize Comfort and Functionality:* When organizing your space, prioritize comfort and functionality. Arrange furniture in a way that promotes relaxation and social interaction. Consider the flow of the room and ensure that pathways are clear and unobstructed. Keep frequently used items easily accessible, while storing less-used items in designated areas. By creating a functional and comfortable layout, you enhance the overall hygge experience.

- *Incorporate Cozy Containers:* Infuse hygge into your organization by incorporating cozy and aesthetically pleasing containers. Opt for natural materials like woven baskets or wooden boxes to store and organize items. These containers add warmth and texture to your space while keeping things tidy. Choose containers that spark joy and resonate with your personal sense of hygge.

- *Integrate Personal Touches:* While decluttering, keep space for personal touches that evoke joy and a sense of connection. Display cherished mementos, family photographs, or artwork that resonates with your hygge aesthetic. These personalized items add warmth, personality, and a sense of belonging to your space.

- *Practice Regular Maintenance:* To maintain a hygge-inspired space, develop a habit of regular maintenance. Set aside time each week to declutter and tidy up. By addressing clutter promptly and consistently, you prevent it from accumulating and disrupting the cozy atmosphere you've created.

Remember, the goal is to create a space that is not only visually appealing but also promotes a sense of comfort, well-being, and relaxation. By decluttering and organizing with the hygge philosophy in mind, you create an environment that supports a cozy and inviting atmosphere, allowing you to fully embrace the joys of hygge in your everyday life.

Here are some additional tips specifically focused on decluttering and organizing spaces that you could find useful to create your hygge space:

Embrace Vertical Harmony. Elevate your organization by utilizing the gentle embrace of vertical storage. Adorn your walls with shelves that rise like comforting arms, hanging organizers that dance with whimsy, or pegboards that offer a symphony of possibilities. Let your belongings find solace in these lofty spaces, allowing surfaces to breathe freely, unburdened by the weight of clutter.

Categorize and Savor. Embark on a journey of mindful curation as you sort your treasures into soulful categories: the garments that wrap you in warmth, the books that nourish your spirit, the utensils that orchestrate culinary delights. Delve deep into each group, seeking the items that spark joy and bring solace to your hygge haven. Tenderly release those that have fulfilled their purpose, allowing them to find new homes where they may find renewed appreciation.

Unveil Serene Sanctuaries. Within the sacred embrace of your abode, designate serene sanctuaries for the various facets of your being. Carve out a nook where inspiration flows, adorned with a desk that whispers of creativity and a chair that cradles your dreams. Create a corner of repose, where plush cushions invite you to surrender to blissful relaxation. Let there be an oasis of order, a storage sanctuary where each possession finds its rightful place, soothing the senses with an organizational symphony.

Cultivate Balance in Flow. As you invite new treasures into your hygge haven, honor the gentle ebb and flow of possessions with the one-in-one-out rule. For every cherished addition that finds its home within these walls, bid farewell to another, releasing it with gratitude and grace. In this delicate dance of equilibrium, your space remains harmonious, open to the joys that await, and free from the burdens of excess.

Secrets Unveiled in Hidden Abodes. Seek refuge in the artful concealment of hidden storage solutions. Discover the mysteries held beneath your bed, where containers cradle memories and dreams. Embrace ottomans with secret compartments, where treasures are tucked away from prying eyes. Let your furniture become guardians of order, concealing their storage prowess beneath their elegant exteriors.

Practice Regular Decluttering like Rituals of Renewal to nurture. Set aside sacred moments, be they weekly or monthly, to embark on the tranquil journey of decluttering and reorganization. During these cherished rituals, let your space be bathed in gentle light and fragrant scents, inviting you to engage in this act of self-care. Assess your belongings with a discerning eye, allowing only those that speak to your heart and align with the hygge spirit to remain. In this rhythmic dance of renewal, your sanctuary remains a haven of serenity and rejuvenation.

Embrace the Art of Clear Surfaces. Resist the temptation to burden your surfaces with the weight of everyday life. Let countertops and tables become canvases of calm, adorned only with the essentials that invite comfort and joy. Allow space for spontaneity and serendipity, where moments of hygge can unfurl like the delicate petals of a blossom.

Foster Generosity in Release. When the time comes to part with belongings that no longer serve your journey, let your heart guide your actions. Embrace the spirit of generosity, whether through donations that kindle hope in the hearts of others or by inviting new stories to unfold through the act of selling. May each possession find its place in the grand tapestry of existence, weaving new tales of comfort and joy.

Remember that the journey of decluttering and organizing your space is a continuous process, a dance of perpetual growth and transformation. Embrace these gentle whispers of guidance as you embark on this hygge-inspired path, allowing the essence of simplicity, serenity, and cherished contentment to permeate your surroundings. By integrating these tips into your daily life, you create a harmonious and clutter-free environment that reflects the core principles of hygge. So, let us embrace the beauty of simplicity, the comfort of a well-organized space, and the contentment that comes from living in alignment with the hygge philosophy.

I would like to share with you some practical tips specifically designed to help you organize your space in alignment with the principles of hygge. These tips strike a balance between decluttering and creating a cozy atmosphere without overcrowding. While they may seem repetitive based on the principles we discussed earlier in this chapter, they are practical actions that you can immediately apply to transform your surroundings according to the hygge principles we have explored. By keeping your environment well decluttered, warm, cozy, and joyful, these tips will help you create a harmonious and hygge-inspired living space.

1. *Embrace Cozy Storage Solutions:* Opt for storage solutions that align with the cozy and inviting atmosphere of hygge. Choose baskets, fabric bins, or wooden crates to store and organize items. These natural materials add warmth and texture to your space while keeping belongings neatly tucked away.

2. *Focus on Essential Items:* When decluttering, prioritize keeping items that align with the hygge lifestyle. Embrace the philosophy of simplicity and let go of excess belongings that don't bring you joy or serve a purpose in creating a cozy and comfortable environment.

3. *Create Hygge Nooks:* Designate cozy nooks within your space where you can relax and indulge in hygge activities. Whether it's a reading corner with a comfortable chair and a small bookshelf or a meditation area with soft

cushions and candles, having these dedicated spaces encourages mindfulness and enhances the hygge experience.

4. *Preserve Sentimental Items:* While decluttering, consider the sentimental value of certain items. Hygge embraces the importance of nostalgia and connections. Keep meaningful possessions that evoke positive memories and incorporate them into your decor, displaying them with intention and care.

5. *Enhance Soft Textures:* Utilize soft textures as a way to organize and add hygge elements to your space. Incorporate cozy blankets or cushions into your storage solutions, such as folding them neatly in baskets or arranging them on shelves. This not only keeps them organized but also adds visual and tactile comfort.

6. *Opt for Warm Lighting:* Choose warm and soft lighting options to create a cozy ambiance. Use lamps with warm-toned bulbs or add fairy lights to your storage areas to create a gentle and inviting glow. Lighting plays a significant role in setting a hygge atmosphere and can enhance the overall cozy feel of your organized space.

7. *Incorporate Nature-Inspired Organization:* Bring elements of nature into your organizational systems. Use

small potted plants as decorative accents on shelves or incorporate natural materials like woven grass or rattan baskets. This connection with nature adds a calming and grounding element to your space.

8. *Practice Mindful Decluttering:* Approach the decluttering process with a mindful mindset. Take the time to reflect on the items you have and carefully decide what truly brings you joy and aligns with the hygge philosophy. Mindful decluttering allows you to create a space that is intentional, peaceful, and filled with items that enhance your well-being.

Start incorporating these hygge-inspired decluttering and organizing tips right away to create a space that promotes a sense of calm and comfort while reflecting the principles of hygge. By doing so, you will immediately begin to enjoy all the benefits that come with embracing a hygge lifestyle.

Chapter 3: Hygge in Relationships and Social Interactions

How Hygge Can Strengthen Connections and Foster Intimacy

In our fast-paced and interconnected world, it's easy to overlook the importance of genuine connections and intimate moments in our relationships. Hygge has the power to transform the way we nurture our relationships, fostering a deeper sense of intimacy and strengthening the bonds we share with our loved ones. It encourages us to slow down, create inviting spaces, and cultivate meaningful experiences that prioritize quality time and heartfelt connections. By embracing the principles of hygge, we can create a sanctuary of warmth, understanding, and love, where authentic connections flourish and intimacy thrives. In this chapter, we will explore how hygge can enhance our relationships, providing practical tips and inspiring insights on how to infuse hygge into our lives to cultivate deeper connections with our partners, family, and friends.

Hygge has the remarkable ability to strengthen connections and foster intimacy in relationships. Here's how hygge can create a nurturing and intimate environment:

Quality Time

Hygge emphasizes the value of quality time spent with loved ones. By embracing hygge, we prioritize meaningful interactions and create intentional spaces where we can truly connect. Whether it's sharing a meal, engaging in heartfelt conversations, or simply enjoying each other's company in a cozy setting, hygge encourages us to be present and attentive to the people around us.

Cozy Gatherings

Creating a cozy and inviting atmosphere is at the core of hygge. By curating spaces that exude warmth and comfort, we create an environment that encourages relaxation and openness. Whether it's hosting intimate gatherings with friends or spending quiet evenings with a partner, the cozy ambiance fosters a sense of closeness, allowing for genuine conversations, shared laughter, and the building of deeper connections.

Authenticity and Vulnerability

Hygge invites us to be authentic and embrace vulnerability within our relationships. In a hygge setting, we can let down our guards, be our true selves, and share our thoughts, emotions, and experiences without judgment. This sense of safety and acceptance nurtures trust and strengthens the bonds between individuals, fostering deeper connections and a stronger sense of intimacy.

Mindful Presence

Hygge encourages us to be fully present and engaged in the moment, especially when in the company of others. By practicing mindfulness and setting aside distractions, we show our loved ones that they have our undivided attention and that they are valued. This mindful presence creates a space where meaningful connections can flourish and allows for a deeper understanding and appreciation of one another.

Rituals and Traditions

Hygge embraces the power of rituals and traditions in creating a sense of belonging and shared experiences. By establishing hygge-inspired rituals within relationships, such as weekly game nights, Sunday brunches, or cozy movie marathons, we create a sense of continuity and anticipation. These rituals become cherished traditions that strengthen the bond between individuals and provide opportunities for creating lasting memories.

Gratitude and Appreciation

Hygge encourages us to cultivate gratitude and appreciation for the simple joys and the presence of our loved ones. By expressing gratitude and acknowledging the positive qualities and actions of those around us, we deepen our connection and foster an environment of love and appreciation. This fosters a sense of intimacy and strengthens the foundation of our relationships.

Unplugging and Digital Detox

Hygge encourages us to disconnect from the digital world and be fully present with our loved ones. By creating technology-free zones or designated periods of digital detox, we can devote uninterrupted time to nurturing our relationships. This intentional break from screens allows for deeper conversations, increased eye contact, and genuine connection, fostering intimacy in our interactions.

Shared Experiences in Nature

Hygge embraces the beauty of nature and encourages us to incorporate it into our relationships. Spending time outdoors together, whether it's going for walks in the park, having a picnic in a scenic spot, or enjoying a bonfire under the starry sky, can create meaningful shared experiences. The tranquility and beauty of nature provide a backdrop for connection, introspection, and appreciating the wonders of the world together.

Acts of Kindness and Thoughtfulness

Hygge emphasizes the importance of small gestures and acts of kindness. Engaging in thoughtful actions, such as surprising a loved one with their favorite treat, writing a heartfelt note, or simply lending a listening ear, deepens the bond between individuals. These acts of kindness show care, empathy, and thoughtfulness, creating an atmosphere of warmth and fostering a sense of intimacy.

Embracing Imperfections

Hygge encourages us to embrace imperfections and celebrate the authenticity of our relationships. By letting go of unrealistic expectations and accepting each other's flaws, we create a safe space where individuals can be their true selves. This vulnerability and acceptance strengthen connections, as it allows for open and honest communication, creating a deeper sense of intimacy.

Intimate Dinners and Hygge Hospitality

Hygge places great importance on shared meals and the concept of hygge hospitality. Hosting intimate dinners or cozy gatherings at home, where delicious food is prepared and enjoyed together, fosters a sense of togetherness and intimacy. The act of breaking bread and sharing nourishment strengthens the bonds between individuals, creating a warm and inviting atmosphere.

Mindful Listening and Empathy

Hygge teaches us the art of mindful listening and empathetic understanding. By truly listening to others without judgment and seeking to understand their perspectives and emotions, we create space for deeper connection and intimacy. Offering support, empathy, and validation to our loved ones strengthens the trust and intimacy within relationships.

Hygge reminds us to slow down, savor the moments, and nurture the relationships that bring us joy and comfort. By incorporating hygge principles into our social interactions, we create a space where connections can flourish, vulnerability is embraced, and intimacy is nurtured. It's through the practice of hygge that we can strengthen our relationships and cultivate a deep sense of closeness with those who matter most to us.

The Importance of Meaningful Conversations, Quality Time, and Shared Experiences

Meaningful conversations, quality time, and shared experiences are essential elements of hygge philosophy and lifestyle. In the hustle and bustle of modern life, we often find ourselves caught up in a flurry of distractions, leaving little time for meaningful conversations and quality connections with our loved ones. Hygge reminds us of the importance of slowing down and creating intentional spaces for heartfelt conversations. By carving out dedicated time to engage in genuine and meaningful discussions, we deepen our understanding of one another and strengthen the bonds we share.

Hygge also emphasizes the significance of quality time spent together. It encourages us to put aside our devices and be fully present in the company of our loved ones. Whether it's enjoying a cozy meal, engaging in a shared hobby, or simply cuddling up on the couch, hygge teaches us to savor these moments and cherish the time we have together. Quality time allows us to connect on a deeper level, fostering a sense of closeness, trust, and intimacy.

Shared experiences form the fabric of our relationships, creating lasting memories and a sense of belonging. Hygge invites us to create opportunities for shared experiences that bring joy, laughter, and connection. It can be as simple as taking a walk in nature, playing board games, or embarking on a weekend getaway. These shared experiences build a shared narrative and strengthen the bonds between individuals, creating a sense of togetherness and cultivating deeper connections.

Hygge emphasizes the art of active listening, which involves giving our full attention to the person we are engaging with. It means setting aside distractions, maintaining eye contact, and truly listening to understand rather than simply waiting for our turn to speak. Active listening fosters a deeper connection by demonstrating genuine interest and empathy, making the other person feel seen, heard, and valued.

Hygge encourages the creation of rituals and traditions within our relationships. These can be simple, everyday rituals such as having a morning coffee together, cooking a meal as a team, or having a weekly movie night. Rituals provide a sense of continuity, stability, and anticipation, strengthening the bond between individuals and creating shared memories.

Hygge creates a safe space for vulnerability within relationships. It encourages open and honest communication, allowing individuals to express their thoughts, feelings, and fears without judgment. By embracing vulnerability, we foster a deeper sense of trust and connection, as we are able to truly be ourselves and be accepted for who we are.

Hygge promotes an attitude of gratitude and appreciation within relationships. It encourages us to express gratitude for the small joys and moments we share with our loved ones. This practice cultivates a positive and nurturing environment, where appreciation for one another becomes an integral part of the relationship, strengthening the connection and fostering a sense of well-being.

While quality time together is important, hygge also recognizes the significance of individual alone time. It's crucial to strike a balance between spending time together and respecting each other's need for solitude and self-reflection. Allowing space for personal growth and rejuvenation supports healthy relationships and enhances the appreciation and enjoyment of the time spent together.

By embracing meaningful conversations, quality time, and shared experiences, hygge enables us to nurture our relationships and enhance our overall well-being. It encourages us to prioritize the people who matter most to us, creating a warm and inviting space where heartfelt connections can flourish. Through these intentional acts, hygge allows us to build deeper relationships, foster intimacy, and create a sense of belonging that brings comfort and fulfillment to our lives.

Suggestions for Incorporating Hygge into Gatherings, Celebrations, and Everyday Interactions with Loved Ones

Imagine a warm and inviting atmosphere, where cherished moments are shared, laughter fills the air, and connections are deepened. This is the essence of hygge. By incorporating hygge into our gatherings, celebrations, and daily interactions with loved ones, we can create an environment that nurtures deep connections, fosters intimacy, and cultivates a sense of contentment. Whether it's a cozy dinner party with friends, a holiday celebration with family, or a quiet evening spent with a loved one, embracing hygge allows us to savor the present moment, cherish meaningful interactions, and create lasting memories. In this section, we will explore practical tips and ideas, taken from the principles shared in the previous part of this chapter, for infusing hygge into our social engagements, enabling us to enhance our relationships, find comfort in each other's presence, and create a sanctuary of warmth and joy.

Here are some suggestions for incorporating hygge into gatherings, celebrations, and everyday interactions with loved ones:

Create a Cozy Atmosphere: Set the mood by creating a cozy and inviting atmosphere. Use soft lighting, such as candles or fairy lights, to create a warm ambiance. Arrange comfortable seating with plush pillows and blankets to encourage relaxation and coziness.

Embrace Slow-Paced Gatherings: Encourage a slow-paced and relaxed gathering by setting aside ample time for conversation and connection. Avoid rushing through activities and allow for spontaneous conversations to unfold. Emphasize quality over quantity, focusing on meaningful interactions rather than a packed schedule.

Serve Comforting and Nourishing Food: Hygge gatherings often feature homemade, comforting, and nourishing food. Prepare dishes that evoke a sense of warmth and comfort, such as soups, stews, baked goods, or hot beverages. Involve your loved ones in the cooking process to create a collaborative and enjoyable experience.

Engage in Shared Activities: Plan activities that foster togetherness and create shared memories. This can include board games, movie nights, nature walks, or crafting sessions. The key is to engage in activities that allow everyone to participate, have fun, and connect on a deeper level.

Practice Mindful Presence: Be fully present during gatherings and interactions with loved ones. Put away distractions such as phones and laptops, and focus on engaging with each other. Practice active listening, show genuine interest, and offer support and understanding.

Celebrate Simple Joys: Find joy in the simple things and celebrate everyday moments. Whether it's enjoying a cup of tea together, watching a sunset, or sharing laughter over funny stories, embrace the beauty of the present moment and find gratitude in the small joys of life.

Emphasize Meaningful Traditions: Incorporate meaningful traditions into your gatherings and celebrations. These can be passed down through generations or created anew. Traditions add a sense of continuity and provide a framework for connection and shared experiences.

Create Hygge Rituals: Establish rituals that promote connection and well-being in everyday interactions. This could include having a morning coffee together, enjoying a family dinner, or practicing a bedtime routine that encourages relaxation and reflection. Rituals provide a sense of structure and create opportunities for regular moments of hygge.

Create a Hygge Playlist: Curate a playlist of soothing and comforting music that sets the mood for relaxation and togetherness. Choose songs that evoke positive emotions and create a cozy atmosphere, allowing everyone to unwind and enjoy the moment.

Incorporate Nature: Connect with nature during gatherings by incorporating natural elements into the environment. Bring in fresh flowers, potted plants, or branches from the outdoors to add a touch of nature to the space. Consider hosting gatherings outdoors or arranging picnics in scenic locations.

Practice Gratitude Rituals: Begin or end gatherings with a gratitude ritual where everyone takes turns expressing what they are grateful for. This practice cultivates a positive and appreciative mindset, fostering a sense of warmth and connection.

Share Stories and Memories: Encourage storytelling by inviting everyone to share meaningful stories, memories, or anecdotes. This can be centered around a theme or simply a time for each person to share a personal story. This activity promotes connection, understanding, and a sense of shared history.

Introduce Hygge-inspired Activities: Incorporate activities that align with hygge principles. For example, host a cozy movie night, organize a DIY craft session, or gather for a book club where you discuss and share your favorite reads. These activities create opportunities for shared experiences and deepen connections.

Create a Hygge Corner: Designate a specific area in your home as a hygge corner, where you can gather with loved ones for intimate conversations and relaxation. Arrange comfortable seating, soft lighting, and include items that bring joy and comfort, such as books, cozy blankets, or a collection of favorite board games.

Embrace Hygge Outdoors: Extend hygge beyond the confines of your home by organizing outdoor activities that promote connection and well-being. This could include bonfires, camping trips, picnics, or nature walks. Embrace the beauty of the natural environment and engage in activities that allow everyone to unwind and enjoy each other's company.

Remember, the essence of incorporating hygge into gatherings, celebrations, and everyday interactions is to prioritize meaningful connections, create a cozy and welcoming environment, and savor the simple pleasures of togetherness. By infusing these practices into your interactions with loved ones, you will create an environment that fosters connection, relaxation, and a sense of well-being, allowing you and your loved ones to truly enjoy each other's company and create lasting memories.

Chapter 4: Embracing Hygge in Self-Care and Mindfulness

The Role of Hygge in Self-Care Practices and Nurturing One's Well-Being

In the hustle and bustle of our modern lives, it's essential to carve out moments of tranquility and prioritize our well-being. This is where hygge comes into play. Hygge offers a gentle reminder to slow down, find comfort in simple pleasures, and cultivate a nurturing relationship with ourselves. It encompasses self-care practices that not only pamper our physical and emotional needs but also foster a deep sense of well-being. From creating a cozy sanctuary to savoring the small joys in life, hygge invites us to embrace self-care as a fundamental aspect of nurturing our overall well-being. By incorporating hygge into our daily lives, we can cultivate a harmonious balance, find solace in self-reflection, and create a sanctuary that supports our journey of self-discovery and contentment.

Hygge holds a significant role in self-care, nurturing our well-being and fostering a harmonious relationship with ourselves. By embracing hygge in our self-care practices, we create a nurturing and fulfilling connection with our inner selves. It encourages us to embrace the present moment, savor simple joys, and establish a comforting environment that supports our overall well-being. Prioritizing self-care becomes an integral part of our daily lives, allowing us to cultivate inner peace, contentment, and a deeper sense of well-being. Let's explore how we can incorporate hygge into our self-care and well-being routines.

Creating a Sanctuary

Hygge encourages the creation of a cozy and comforting environment that serves as a sanctuary for self-care. By surrounding ourselves with soft blankets, calming scents, warm lighting, and soothing textures, we can create a space where we can retreat and rejuvenate.

Embracing Mindfulness

Hygge emphasizes the practice of mindfulness and embracing the simple pleasures of life, allowing us to fully immerse ourselves in the present moment. By slowing down and engaging our senses, we can appreciate the beauty and tranquility of our surroundings, experiencing a profound sense of calm and alleviating stress and anxiety. In the following sections of this chapter, we will delve further into the connection between hygge, mindfulness, and their role in self-care practices and personal well-being.

Nurturing Routines

Hygge encourages the development of nurturing routines that prioritize self-care. Whether it's starting the day with a cup of tea, enjoying a relaxing bath in the evening, or having a designated time for reading or practicing a hobby, these rituals provide a sense of comfort, stability, and self-indulgence.

Finding Joy in Small Moments

Hygge reminds us to find joy in the simple moments of everyday life. It's about relishing a warm sip of hot cocoa, curling up with a good book, or savoring a homemade meal. By focusing on these small pleasures, we cultivate gratitude, contentment, and a heightened sense of well-being.

Embracing Hygge Hygiene

Hygge hygiene involves taking care of ourselves physically, emotionally, and mentally. This includes prioritizing restful sleep, nourishing our bodies with wholesome foods, engaging in activities that bring us joy and relaxation, and nurturing our relationships with loved ones.

Cultivating Connection

Hygge encourages nurturing meaningful connections with others, which is essential for our overall well-being. Spending quality time with loved ones, engaging in heartfelt conversations, and participating in shared activities foster a sense of belonging, love, and support.

Balancing Solitude and Socializing

Hygge recognizes the importance of finding a balance between solitude and socializing. Taking time for ourselves to recharge and reflect is just as important as engaging in social interactions. By honoring our need for alone time and meaningful social connections, we cultivate a sense of self-awareness and fulfillment.

Prioritizing Comfort

Hygge embraces the concept of comfort as a central pillar of self-care. This includes cozy clothing, soft blankets, comfortable furniture, and anything that promotes physical and emotional well-being. By prioritizing our comfort, we create an environment that supports relaxation, rejuvenation, and a deep sense of self-care.

Embracing Hygge in Personal Rituals

Hygge encourages the integration of comforting rituals into our self-care practices. Whether it's starting the day with a quiet meditation, enjoying a leisurely morning routine, or winding down with a calming bedtime ritual, incorporating hygge elements into these personal rituals enhances their soothing and nurturing effects.

Savoring Simple Pleasures

Hygge invites us to savor the simple pleasures in life. It could be as uncomplicated as indulging in a piece of homemade cake, taking a leisurely stroll in nature, or spending time with a beloved pet. By being fully present in these moments and relishing their beauty, we cultivate a sense of joy and well-being.

Embracing Hygge-inspired Self-Care Activities

Hygge encourages engaging in activities that promote relaxation and well-being. This could include practicing gentle yoga, journaling, creating art, or enjoying a hot bath with soothing essential oils. These activities nourish our mind, body, and soul, allowing us to recharge and find inner balance.

Incorporating Hygge Elements in Personal Space

Infusing our personal space with hygge elements can significantly contribute to our well-being. Adding soft cushions and throws, using warm and inviting lighting, incorporating natural elements like plants, and displaying cherished mementos all create a comforting and personalized environment that supports our self-care practices.

Hygge as a Mindset

Beyond the physical aspects, hygge is also a mindset that embraces self-compassion, self-acceptance, and the permission to prioritize our well-being. It encourages us to let go of perfectionism and the need for constant productivity, allowing ourselves to simply be and enjoy the present moment without judgment.

Nurturing Relationships with Ourselves

Hygge reminds us to cultivate a loving and compassionate relationship with ourselves. This involves practicing self-care, setting boundaries, honoring our needs and desires, and treating ourselves with kindness and understanding. By nurturing our relationship with ourselves, we build a foundation of self-love and resilience.

Hygge as a Sustainable Practice

Hygge promotes sustainability and conscious living as integral components of self-care. It encourages us to appreciate and care for the environment, make mindful consumption choices, and create a living space that aligns with our values of simplicity and harmony. By living in harmony with nature, we contribute to our own well-being and the well-being of the planet.

Incorporating these additional aspects into our understanding of hygge and its role in self-care practices enhances our ability to nurture our well-being, find inner peace, and create a fulfilling and balanced life. By embracing hygge as a holistic approach to self-care, we foster a deep sense of comfort, contentment, and harmony within ourselves.

Mindfulness Techniques and How They Relate to Hygge

In the quest for finding peace and contentment in our fast-paced lives, the concept of hygge and the practice of mindfulness intersect beautifully. Hygge, with its focus on creating cozy, comforting environments and nurturing connections, harmonizes seamlessly with the principles of mindfulness that encourage present-moment awareness and cultivating inner calm. By combining the warmth and simplicity of hygge with the grounded mindfulness practices, we can create a harmonious and deeply fulfilling way of living. This powerful synergy allows us to fully embrace the present moment, appreciate the beauty in the simple things, and nurture our well-being on a profound level. In this section, we will explore the profound relationship between hygge and mindfulness, discovering how they support each other in creating a life of tranquility, gratitude, and inner peace.

Mindfulness techniques play a significant role in the hygge philosophy as they encourage being fully present in the moment and cultivating a sense of peace and contentment. Here are some main mindfulness techniques and points to consider when exploring the relation between mindfulness and hygge:

- *Mindful Breathing:* Focusing on the breath is a foundational mindfulness practice. In hygge, taking slow, deep breaths and being aware of each inhale and exhale helps to ground us in the present moment. It brings a sense of calm and relaxation, allowing us to fully immerse ourselves in the cozy atmosphere and appreciate the simple joys surrounding us.

- *Sensory Awareness:* Hygge encourages us to engage our senses fully and appreciate the present moment's sensory experiences. Mindfulness practices such as mindful eating, where we savor each bite and pay attention to the taste, texture, and aroma of the food, align with hygge's emphasis on enjoying comforting meals and treats mindfully.

- *Body Scan Meditation:* This mindfulness practice involves bringing attention to different parts of the body, noticing sensations, and releasing tension. Incorporating a body scan meditation into hygge allows us to relax and connect with our physical bodies, promoting a sense of comfort and well-being. It helps us tune in to our bodies' needs and create an environment that supports relaxation and coziness.

- *Gratitude Practice:* Practicing gratitude is an integral part of both mindfulness and hygge. Taking time to reflect on and appreciate the simple pleasures and blessings in our lives aligns with hygge's focus on finding joy in everyday moments. Mindfully expressing gratitude for the cozy atmosphere, the warmth of loved ones' presence, and the small comforts of our surroundings amplifies the feeling of contentment and well-being.

- *Mindful Communication:* Hygge emphasizes the value of meaningful connections with loved ones, and mindful communication complements this aspect. Engaging in mindful listening, speaking with intention, and being fully present in conversations foster a deeper sense of connection and understanding. By bringing mindfulness to our interactions, we create a space of warmth and openness, enhancing the hygge experience.

- *Meditation and Reflection:* Incorporating regular meditation or reflection practices into our hygge routine allows us to cultivate a sense of inner peace and self-awareness. Taking time for quiet introspection, journaling, or practicing mindfulness meditation helps us connect with our emotions, thoughts, and desires. It supports our journey of self-discovery, enhancing our overall well-being and ability to create a hygge-inspired life.

- *Mindful Movement:* Engaging in gentle, mindful movement practices such as yoga, walking in nature, or even slow stretching can complement the hygge lifestyle. By bringing awareness to our bodies' movements, we can deepen our connection with ourselves and create a sense of ease and relaxation. Mindful movement can be a way to release tension, increase body awareness, and enhance the overall sense of well-being.

- *Digital Detox:* In today's digital age, it's important to carve out time for unplugging and disconnecting from screens. Incorporating digital detoxes into the hygge lifestyle allows us to create space for mindfulness and be fully present in our surroundings. By setting aside designated periods without digital distractions, we can engage in activities that promote relaxation, connection, and self-care.

- *Mindful Appreciation:* Hygge encourages us to cultivate an attitude of appreciation and mindfulness in all aspects of life. Taking moments throughout the day to pause, observe, and appreciate the beauty around us fosters a deeper sense of gratitude and contentment. It can be as simple as noticing the warmth of a cup of tea, the softness of a blanket, or the beauty of nature outside our window.

- *Mindful Rituals:* Infusing mindfulness into daily rituals can elevate the hygge experience. Whether it's preparing a comforting meal, brewing a cup of tea, or lighting candles, approaching these activities with mindful awareness enhances the sense of coziness and presence. By slowing down, engaging our senses, and being fully present in these rituals, we create a deeper connection to ourselves and the present moment.

Remember, the essence of hygge lies in cultivating a sense of comfort, contentment, and mindful awareness. Incorporating mindfulness techniques into your hygge practice enhances your ability to fully immerse yourself in the cozy atmosphere, connect with loved ones, and nurture your own well-being. These practices empower you to create a harmonious balance between inner peace and the external environment, resulting in a more fulfilling and hyggelig life.

Suggestions and Ideas for Incorporating Hygge into Relaxation Rituals, Self-Reflection, and Embracing Solitude

In the midst of our fast-paced and often hectic lives, finding moments of peace, self-reflection, and connection with ourselves is essential for our well-being. Hygge teaches us to embrace relaxation rituals, engage in self-reflection, and cherish solitude as precious opportunities to nurture our souls and enhance our overall sense of well-being. By incorporating hygge into our lives, we create space for comfort, mindfulness, and deep connection with ourselves. In this section, we will explore various ways to infuse hygge into our relaxation rituals, engage in self-reflection practices, and fully embrace the beauty of solitude. Get ready for some practical action. You will create a sanctuary of calm and contentment within your daily life, where you can find solace, inner peace, and a renewed sense of self.

Here are some practical ideas for incorporating hygge into relaxation rituals, self-reflection, and embracing solitude:

Cozy Reading Nook

Create a cozy reading nook in your home where you can retreat to embrace solitude and indulge in your favorite books. Include soft pillows, a warm blanket, and a comfortable chair or bean bag. Dim the lights, light some candles, and enjoy a cup of hot tea or cocoa while you immerse yourself in a good book.

Hygge Bathing Ritual

Transform your bathing experience into a hygge-inspired ritual of relaxation. Fill your bathroom with soft lighting, soothing music, and scented candles. Add luxurious bath oils or bath salts to the water, and take your time to soak and unwind. Embrace the feeling of warmth and comfort as you indulge in this self-care practice.

Mindful Journaling

Set aside time for self-reflection through mindful journaling. Find a quiet and comfortable space where you can freely express your thoughts and emotions on paper. Reflect on your day, jot down gratitude lists, or explore your dreams and aspirations. Embrace the solitude and allow your thoughts to flow without judgment.

Nature Walks

Connect with the beauty of nature by taking solitary walks in parks, forests, or gardens. Pay attention to the sights, sounds, and scents around you. Allow yourself to be present in the moment, taking in the tranquility and embracing the soothing effect of nature. Dress warmly, if needed, and feel the crisp air on your skin as you immerse yourself in the serenity of the outdoors.

Hygge-inspired Craft or Hobby

Engage in a craft or hobby that brings you joy and helps you embrace solitude. Whether it's knitting, painting, baking, or playing a musical instrument, find an activity that allows you to focus and unwind. Create a dedicated space in your home for pursuing your craft, filled with cozy elements such as soft lighting, comfortable seating, and inspiring artwork.

Mindful Meditation

Practice mindfulness meditation as a way to embrace solitude and foster inner calm. Set aside dedicated time each day to sit in a quiet space, close your eyes, and focus on your breath. Allow your thoughts to come and go without judgment, gently bringing your attention back to your breath. Embrace the stillness and cultivate a sense of peace within.

Hygge-inspired Aromatherapy

Create a soothing atmosphere by incorporating hygge-inspired aromatherapy. Use essential oils such as lavender, chamomile, or vanilla in a diffuser or mix them with carrier oils for a relaxing massage. The gentle scent will help you unwind, reduce stress, and enhance your sense of well-being.

Hygge Tea Time

Set aside time for a cozy tea ritual where you can enjoy a warm cup of herbal tea or your favorite beverage. Use beautiful, comforting mugs or teacups and create a serene ambiance with soft music, dim lighting, and perhaps a delicious treat to accompany your tea. Allow yourself to savor each sip and embrace the moment of quiet indulgence.

Mindful Gratitude Practice

Embrace self-reflection and gratitude by incorporating a mindful gratitude practice into your routine. Each day, take a few moments to reflect on and write down things you are grateful for. Focus on the simple joys, moments of connection, and blessings in your life. This practice cultivates a sense of appreciation and contentment, fostering a hygge-inspired mindset.

Digital Detox Retreat

Designate a day or weekend for a digital detox retreat. Disconnect from technology and immerse yourself in activities that promote relaxation and self-care. Spend time reading, practicing yoga, taking nature walks, journaling, or engaging in hobbies without the distractions of screens. Embrace the freedom from constant connectivity and allow yourself to fully embrace the present moment.

Cozy Solo Dinners

Create a hygge-inspired solo dining experience by preparing a comforting meal for yourself. Set a beautiful table with soft lighting, a cozy tablecloth, and your favorite dishes. Cook a nourishing meal and savor each bite mindfully. Use this time to connect with your senses, enjoy the flavors, and appreciate the act of nourishing yourself.

Creative Expression

Engage in creative activities that allow you to express yourself and embrace solitude. Paint, draw, write, dance, or play a musical instrument. Let go of judgment and focus on the joy and freedom of creative expression. Allow yourself to be fully present in the process and embrace the therapeutic benefits of engaging in artistic endeavors.

Remember, the essence of incorporating hygge into relaxation rituals, self-reflection, and embracing solitude is to create an environment and mindset that nourishes your well-being. Choose activities and practices that resonate with you personally and bring you a sense of comfort, tranquility, and joy. Embrace these moments of solitude as opportunities for self-care and rejuvenation, and savor the peace that hygge can bring to your life.

Chapter 5: Hygge Across Seasons and Celebrations

How Hygge Can Be Adapted to Different Seasons and Festivities

Step into a world where celebrations and seasons are embraced with warmth, togetherness, and a cozy ambiance. Hygge permeates through the festive traditions and changing seasons. Whether it's the enchanting glow of Christmas lights, the crackling bonfires of Midsummer's Eve, or the vibrant colors of autumn leaves, hygge infuses every celebration and season with a sense of tranquility and contentment. Join me on a journey as we explore how hygge intertwines with celebrations and adapts to the unique qualities of each season, inviting us to cherish the present, connect with loved ones, and create cherished memories in a harmonious and inviting atmosphere.

Hygge can be adapted to different seasons and festivities, allowing us to embrace the unique qualities and joys each season brings. Here are some ways to infuse hygge into different seasons and festivities:

Winter Hygge

Winter is often associated with cozy warmth and a sense of hygge. Embrace the season by creating a warm and inviting atmosphere with soft blankets, flickering candles, and a crackling fireplace. Indulge in hot drinks like mulled wine or hot chocolate and savor comforting winter meals. Enjoy activities such as building snowmen, ice skating, or curling up with a good book by the fire. Winter hygge is all about finding beauty and comfort in the cold season.

Spring Hygge

As nature awakens and blooms, embrace the freshness and renewal of spring. Bring hygge outdoors by having picnics in the park, going for nature walks, or planting flowers in your garden. Enjoy the vibrant colors and scents of blossoming flowers. Invite friends over for a gathering and celebrate the season with a spring-inspired feast. Embrace the feeling of rejuvenation and new beginnings that spring brings.

Summer Hygge

Summer is a time of warmth and outdoor enjoyment. Create a hygge-inspired outdoor oasis by setting up a cozy seating area with comfortable cushions and blankets. Enjoy barbecues, picnics, and al fresco dining with loved ones. Take leisurely walks in the park, go for a swim, or simply bask in the sun's rays. Embrace the slower pace of summer, savoring the long days and warm evenings.

Autumn Hygge

Autumn is a season of change and harvest. Embrace the cozy and nostalgic atmosphere by incorporating warm hues, scented candles, and soft lighting into your home. Indulge in comforting autumnal foods like soups, stews, and apple pie. Go for walks in nature and immerse yourself in the beauty of falling leaves and crisp air. Host gatherings centered around harvest celebrations, pumpkin carving, or cozy movie nights. Autumn hygge is about embracing the beauty of change and finding comfort in the season's charm.

Festive Hygge

Infuse hygge into festive celebrations such as Christmas, Thanksgiving, or other cultural holidays. Create a welcoming ambiance with twinkling lights, festive decorations, and the scent of spices in the air. Gather with loved ones for cozy meals, heartfelt conversations, and the exchange of thoughtful gifts. Embrace traditions that bring joy and foster a sense of togetherness. Festive hygge is about creating cherished memories and finding warmth and connection during special occasions.

By adapting hygge to different seasons and festivities, we can fully embrace the unique qualities and joys that each one offers. It allows us to create meaningful rituals, find comfort in our surroundings, and foster connections with loved ones, all while appreciating the beauty of the changing seasons and celebrating life's special moments. We will delve deeper into this subject further on in this chapter.

In addition to adapting hygge to different seasons and festivities, it's important to consider the specific elements that can enhance the experience during each time of the year. Here are some additional ideas:

Embrace nature

Incorporate natural elements that are abundant during each season. For example, in spring, bring fresh flowers into your home or spend time in blooming gardens. During summer, enjoy outdoor activities surrounded by lush greenery or near bodies of water. In autumn, gather colorful leaves or create cozy outdoor bonfires. In winter, decorate your space with evergreen branches or bring in potted plants for a touch of nature.

Engage your senses

Each season has its unique sensory experiences. Embrace them to deepen your hygge practice. In spring, open your windows to let in the fresh breeze and listen to birds chirping. During summer, indulge in the aroma of blooming flowers or the scent of freshly cut grass. In autumn, savor the crisp air and the smell of fallen leaves. During winter, enjoy the cozy scents of cinnamon, spices, and hot beverages like mulled wine or apple cider.

Seasonal activities

Incorporate seasonal activities that align with the hygge lifestyle. In spring, practice mindfulness while gardening or take leisurely walks in blossoming parks. Summer can be filled with outdoor picnics, barbecues, and starlit evenings. In autumn, engage in cozy indoor activities like baking or crafting. During winter, embrace activities like ice skating, building snowmen, or having cozy movie nights with loved ones.

Culinary delights

Explore seasonal foods and drinks that bring comfort and joy. In each season, focus on ingredients and dishes that are abundant and reflective of the time of year. For example, in spring, incorporate fresh produce into your meals and enjoy lighter, refreshing dishes. During autumn, indulge in warming soups, stews, and pumpkin-inspired treats. In winter, savor hearty comfort foods and hot beverages like cocoa or spiced teas.

Remember, the essence of incorporating hygge into different seasons and festivities is to create an atmosphere of comfort, connection, and mindfulness. By paying attention to the unique qualities of each season, embracing seasonal activities and flavors, and engaging your senses, you can deepen your hygge experience and fully immerse yourself in the beauty and richness of each time of the year.

Denmark is known for its rich cultural traditions and celebrations that often embody the spirit of hygge. While there may not be specific "hygge celebrations" per se, many Danish celebrations and festivities naturally embrace the hygge lifestyle.

Christmas (Jul)

Christmas is a highly anticipated and cherished holiday in Denmark. The Danes take great pleasure in creating a cozy and warm atmosphere during this time. Homes are beautifully decorated with candles, twinkling lights, and ornaments. Families gather to enjoy traditional Danish Christmas foods, exchange gifts, and engage in hygge-inducing activities like baking cookies, making homemade decorations, and singing carols together.

New Year's Eve (Nytårsaften)

Danish New Year's Eve celebrations are often marked by intimate gatherings with close friends and family. People come together to enjoy a festive meal, share stories, and engage in lively conversations. As the clock strikes midnight, fireworks light up the sky, and everyone joins in cheering and wishing each other a happy new year. It's a time for reflection, gratitude, and looking forward to the possibilities that lie ahead.

Midsummer's Eve (Sankt Hans Aften)

Celebrated on the evening of June 23rd, Midsummer's Eve is a popular Danish tradition that combines elements of bonfires, music, and community. People gather around bonfires on beaches or in parks, enjoying the warmth and crackling flames while singing songs and dancing.

It's a festive and convivial occasion that fosters a sense of togetherness and connection.

Hyggekrog

While not necessarily a celebration, the concept of "hyggekrog" is an important element of Danish culture. A hyggekrog refers to a cozy nook or corner in one's home where they can relax, unwind, and find comfort. It may be a reading corner with a plush armchair, a window seat bathed in natural light, or a dedicated space for hobbies. Creating a hyggekrog is a way to personalize and cultivate a space that embodies the essence of hygge in everyday life.

While these celebrations and traditions in Denmark may not be exclusively hygge-themed, they often align with the principles of hygge by emphasizing coziness, togetherness, and creating a warm and welcoming atmosphere. Experiencing these celebrations firsthand in Denmark would provide a deeper understanding and appreciation for the Danish approach to creating a hygge-filled lifestyle. Until you'll get the chance to go and experience them in person, we will explore them in major depth further on in this chapter.

Hygge Practices During Winter, Spring, Summer, and Autumn.

As the seasons change, so does the essence of hygge. Each season presents unique opportunities to embrace the philosophy of hygge and find comfort, joy, and contentment. During winter, hygge thrives in the cozy sanctuaries we create, where soft blankets, warm lighting, and comforting food nourish both our bodies and souls. Spring brings a sense of renewal and invites us to embrace nature's awakening. We can cultivate hygge by surrounding ourselves with fresh flowers, enjoying the gentle warmth of sunlight, and indulging in simple outdoor pleasures. In summer, hygge takes on a more vibrant and lighthearted feel as we savor the longer days and create cherished memories with loved ones. We immerse ourselves in outdoor activities, relish the flavors of seasonal fruits, and find solace in the simplicity of life. Autumn evokes a sense of nostalgia and invites us to slow down and appreciate the beauty of change. We find hygge in cozy sweaters, fragrant spices, and the comfort of being surrounded by nature's vibrant colors. By embracing hygge throughout the seasons, we can truly immerse ourselves in the joys and wonders that each season brings, cultivating a deep connection with ourselves, our surroundings, and the natural rhythms of life. Let's delve deeper into hygge practices during each season.

Winter

Winter is the quintessential season for hygge, as it embraces all things cozy and comforting. Embrace the cold weather by snuggling up under a soft blanket, sipping a warm cup of cocoa, and enjoying the flickering glow of candles. Engage in indoor activities like reading a book, playing board games, or crafting, creating a sense of togetherness with loved ones. Embrace the beauty of winter by taking leisurely walks in nature, feeling the crisp air on your cheeks, and reveling in the peacefulness of a winter wonderland.

Winter is a season that epitomizes hygge with its cozy atmosphere, soft blankets of snow, and warm gatherings. Here are some ways to embrace hygge during the winter season:

- *Create a Cozy Sanctuary:* Winter is the perfect time to transform your home into a cozy sanctuary. Use soft and plush textiles such as faux fur blankets, fluffy pillows, and warm rugs to create a cozy and inviting atmosphere. Add warm lighting with candles, fairy lights, or dimmed lamps to create a soft and comforting ambiance.

- *Enjoy Warm Comfort Food:* Indulge in nourishing and comforting winter dishes. Prepare hearty soups, stews, and roasted meals that fill your home with delicious aromas. Savor a cup of hot cocoa, mulled wine, or a steaming mug of tea while enjoying a good book or spending quality time with loved ones. The warmth and flavors of winter comfort food contribute to a sense of coziness and well-being.

- *Embrace Hygge Hydration:* Hydration is essential during the winter months. Enjoy warm and comforting beverages such as herbal teas, hot water with lemon and honey, or spiced cider. Hygge hydration not only keeps you warm but also nourishes your body and promotes a sense of well-being.

- *Engage in Indoor Activities:* Winter provides the perfect opportunity to engage in indoor activities that bring joy and relaxation. Curl up by the fireplace with a book, watch movies or binge-watch a favorite TV series, or engage in board games or puzzles with family and friends. Embrace activities that foster connection and create warm memories.

- *Embrace Winter Outdoor Adventures:* Despite the colder temperatures, don't shy away from outdoor activities that embrace the beauty of winter. Go for peaceful walks in snowy landscapes, have fun sledding or building snowmen, or indulge in winter sports like skiing or ice skating. The crisp air and breathtaking scenery can invigorate your senses and provide a unique hygge experience.

- *Practice Hygge Self-Care:* Winter is a time to prioritize self-care and well-being. Take soothing baths with scented oils or bath bombs, indulge in moisturizing skincare routines, or practice gentle yoga or meditation. Focus on nourishing your body and mind, and create moments of relaxation and rejuvenation amidst the winter season.

- *Embrace Candlelight and Warmth:* The soft glow of candlelight is particularly enchanting during the winter months. Light candles throughout your home to create a cozy and magical ambiance. Use warm and inviting lighting in each room, opting for softer bulbs or warm-toned LED lights that mimic the glow of a fireplace.

- *Foster Community and Connection:* Winter is a time for coming together and fostering community. Organize gatherings with friends and family, whether it's a cozy dinner party, a game night, or a movie marathon. Share stories, laughter, and good food in an atmosphere of warmth and togetherness.

By embracing these hygge practices during the winter season, you can create a sense of comfort, coziness, and connection. Embrace the beauty of the season, both indoors and outdoors, and allow the spirit of hygge to bring warmth and contentment to your winter experience.

Spring

As the world awakens from its winter slumber, spring brings a renewed sense of energy and joy. Embrace the arrival of spring by opening your windows to let in fresh air and natural light. Take leisurely strolls through blooming gardens, enjoying the vibrant colors and fragrant scents. Engage in outdoor activities like picnics, gardening, or cycling. Embrace the spirit of renewal by decluttering your living space and introducing touches of nature into your home with fresh flowers and potted plants.

Spring is a season of renewal and rejuvenation, and incorporating hygge practices during this time can enhance our appreciation of its unique qualities. Here are some ways to embrace hygge during spring:

- *Embrace Nature's Awakening:* Spring brings forth blooming flowers, budding trees, and vibrant colors. Take the time to immerse yourself in nature's beauty by going for walks in parks, gardens, or countryside areas. Notice the delicate petals, listen to the chirping of birds, and feel the gentle breeze on your skin. Engaging with nature can bring a sense of tranquility and connection to the natural world.

- *Create Outdoor Hygge Spaces:* As the weather becomes milder, create inviting outdoor spaces where you can soak up the sunshine and fresh air. Set up a cozy seating area on your patio or balcony with comfortable cushions, blankets, and perhaps a small table for enjoying meals or beverages outdoors. Surround yourself with potted plants or hang fairy lights to add a touch of enchantment to your outdoor hygge sanctuary.

- *Embrace Lightness and Airiness:* Spring is a time when we bid farewell to the darkness of winter and welcome longer daylight hours. Open up your curtains or blinds to let in as much natural light as possible. Opt for light and airy fabrics in your home decor, such as breezy curtains or lightweight linens. Incorporate pastel colors and fresh, floral patterns to evoke the freshness and vitality of the season.

- *Engage in Spring Cleaning:* Spring cleaning is not only about tidying up your physical space but also decluttering your mind. Take the opportunity to declutter and organize your living spaces, creating a sense of openness and harmony. As you clean, do it mindfully, appreciating the process and the sense of renewal it brings. Donate or recycle items you no longer need, creating a sense of lightness and spaciousness in your surroundings.

- *<u>Celebrate Seasonal Delights:</u>* Embrace the flavors and scents of spring by enjoying seasonal produce and culinary delights. Visit farmers' markets or grow your own herbs and vegetables. Create meals that celebrate the freshness and vibrancy of spring ingredients. Consider hosting picnics or outdoor gatherings with friends and family, enjoying the simple pleasure of good company, delicious food, and the beauty of nature.

By incorporating these hygge practices into your spring routine, you can fully embrace the season of renewal and create a sense of warmth, harmony, and well-being in your daily life. Allow yourself to slow down, appreciate the beauty around you, and find joy in the simplest of spring pleasures.

Summer

Summer invites us to savor the long, sunlit days and embrace the outdoor beauty. Create a hygge atmosphere in the summer by organizing gatherings and barbecues with family and friends. Set up a cozy outdoor seating area with comfortable cushions and blankets, allowing for relaxed conversations and shared laughter. Embrace nature by taking leisurely walks on the beach, swimming in lakes or the sea, and enjoying picnics in picturesque spots. Allow yourself to slow down, indulge in ice cream treats, and bask in the simple pleasures of summer.

Summer is a season of warmth, sunshine, and leisure, and infusing hygge into this vibrant time of year can enhance our enjoyment and relaxation. Here are some ways to embrace hygge during the summer season:

- *Embrace Outdoor Living:* Summer is the perfect time to savor the outdoors and make the most of the longer days. Create cozy outdoor spaces where you can relax, unwind, and connect with nature. Set up comfortable seating areas with soft cushions, outdoor rugs, and shade-providing umbrellas or canopies. Surround yourself with potted plants, blooming flowers, and twinkling lights to create a magical ambiance for evening gatherings.

- *Enjoy Al Fresco Dining:* Take advantage of the pleasant weather by enjoying meals outdoors. Whether it's a picnic in the park, a barbecue in your backyard, or a cozy dinner on the patio, embrace the joy of outdoor dining. Set a beautiful table with natural elements like fresh flowers, use soft lighting with candles or string lights, and savor delicious, seasonal food with loved ones. The combination of good company, delectable meals, and the beauty of nature creates a hygge atmosphere.

- *Seek Natural Escapes:* Use the summer season as an opportunity to explore natural landscapes, whether it's going to the beach, hiking in the mountains, or enjoying a peaceful walk in the forest. Surrounding yourself with the sights, sounds, and scents of nature can provide a deep sense of tranquility and grounding. Allow yourself to fully immerse in the beauty and serenity of the natural world, appreciating the wonders it offers.

- *Embrace Slow, Leisurely Activities:* Summer invites us to slow down and savor the moment. Engage in activities that bring you joy and relaxation, such as reading a book in a hammock, taking leisurely bike rides, practicing yoga or meditation outdoors, or simply lounging in a comfortable chair while listening to your favorite music. Embrace the unhurried pace of summer and prioritize moments of self-care and rejuvenation.

- *Create Refreshing Rituals:* Beat the summer heat by incorporating refreshing rituals into your routine. Indulge in cool treats like homemade ice cream or fruit-infused water. Take soothing baths with fragrant bath oils or spend time near water, whether it's swimming in a pool, taking a dip in the ocean, or simply enjoying a peaceful moment by a lake or river. These rituals can help you stay cool, relaxed, and connected to the pleasures of summer.

By embracing these hygge practices during the summer season, you can fully embrace the carefree and joyful spirit of this time of year. Take the opportunity to savor the beauty of nature, cultivate meaningful connections, and create moments of relaxation and rejuvenation. Allow the warmth of summer to fill your heart and create lasting memories of hygge-filled moments.

Autumn

Autumn, with its golden hues and crisp air, presents a perfect opportunity to embrace hygge. As the leaves change color, bring the warmth of autumn indoors by decorating your home with soft textiles, warm earth tones, and flickering candles. Enjoy the comfort of cozy sweaters and blankets, and indulge in hot beverages like spiced tea or pumpkin-flavored treats. Embrace the season's bounty by visiting farmers' markets, cooking hearty meals, and savoring the flavors of autumn spices. Take leisurely walks in the falling leaves, relishing the beauty of nature's transition.

Autumn, with its crisp air, colorful foliage, and cozy vibes, is a season that naturally lends itself to hygge. Here are some ways to embrace hygge during the autumn season:

- *Embrace Cozy Layers:* As the temperatures begin to cool, it's time to bring out the cozy sweaters, soft blankets, and warm socks. Create a cozy and inviting atmosphere in your home by layering textiles such as plush rugs, soft throw blankets, and comfortable cushions. Use warm, earthy tones and natural materials to add a sense of warmth and comfort to your living spaces.

- *Enjoy Warm Beverages:* Autumn is the perfect time to indulge in warm and comforting beverages. Sip on a cup of hot chocolate, spiced cider, or a soothing herbal tea. Embrace the ritual of preparing these drinks, allowing their comforting aromas to fill your home. Take the time to savor each sip and let it warm both your body and soul.

- *Explore Nature's Beauty:* Autumn is a season of stunning natural beauty, with vibrant foliage and crisp air. Take leisurely walks in parks, forests, or countryside areas to immerse yourself in the sights, sounds, and scents of the season. Collect fallen leaves, acorns, or pinecones to create nature-inspired decorations for your home. Embrace the changing season and appreciate the beauty of transition.

- *Engage in Comforting Activities:* Autumn is a time for slowing down and engaging in comforting activities. Curl up with a good book by the fireplace, indulge in baking aromatic treats like apple pie or pumpkin bread, or gather around the table for a hearty, homemade meal with loved ones. Engage in creative pursuits like knitting, painting, or crafting to express your creativity and embrace the cozy atmosphere.

- *Embrace Candlelight:* As the days become shorter, candlelight becomes even more essential in creating a cozy and intimate ambiance. Fill your home with the warm glow of candles, creating a soothing and inviting atmosphere. Opt for scented candles with fragrances that evoke the essence of autumn, such as cinnamon, vanilla, or woodsy scents. The soft flickering light of candles can enhance a sense of relaxation and intimacy.

- *Practice Mindfulness and Reflection:* Autumn is a season of change and introspection. Take time for self-reflection and mindfulness practices. Journaling, meditation, or simply sitting in quiet contemplation can help you connect with yourself and embrace the changing seasons of life. Use this time to set intentions, express gratitude, and cultivate a sense of inner peace and contentment.

By embracing these hygge practices during the autumn season, you can fully immerse yourself in the cozy and contemplative atmosphere of the season. Embrace the beauty of nature, indulge in comforting rituals, and create a warm and inviting sanctuary in your home. Allow the essence of autumn to inspire a deep sense of hygge in your life.

Remember that by adapting hygge practices to each season, we can fully immerse ourselves in the unique qualities and charms of every time of year. Whether it's finding comfort indoors during the winter, embracing the energy of spring, savoring the joys of summer, or relishing the cozy atmosphere of autumn, hygge allows us to create a sense of harmony and well-being that is attuned to the changing seasons.

The Hygge Traditions Associated with Specific Holidays and Celebrations

Throughout the year, our lives are filled with moments of celebration and joy, and in these special occasions, we have the opportunity to infuse hygge into every detail. From the twinkling lights of Christmas to the laughter-filled gatherings of birthdays, hygge traditions add an extra layer of coziness and connection. It's a time when we gather with loved ones, create memories, and indulge in comforting rituals. Whether it's cozying up by the fire with hot cocoa on a winter evening or sharing a homemade meal around a beautifully set table, hygge traditions invite us to slow down, savor the present moment, and fully embrace the magic and warmth of these celebrations.

Hygge traditions associated with holidays and celebrations bring an extra dose of warmth, coziness, and togetherness to special occasions. These traditions embrace the essence of hygge and create meaningful moments that are cherished and remembered. From Christmas to birthdays, let's explore the hygge traditions associated with specific holidays and celebrations and discover how we can create moments of pure joy, love, and contentment.

Christmas

Christmas is a pinnacle of hygge in Denmark and is celebrated with great warmth and coziness. Families gather around a beautifully decorated Christmas tree, exchange gifts, and indulge in a feast of traditional Danish delicacies. Lighting plays a significant role, with candles illuminating every corner of the home. Hygge is about creating a sense of togetherness, and Danish families often engage in crafting homemade decorations and ornaments, baking cookies, and singing carols together.

So, Christmas is a deeply cherished and special time of year in Denmark, rich with hygge traditions. Here are some ways in which hygge is embraced during the Christmas season:

- *Advent:* The Christmas season begins with the lighting of the Advent wreath on the four Sundays leading up to Christmas. Each Sunday, a candle is lit, marking the countdown to the arrival of Christmas. It creates a cozy atmosphere as families gather together, sing carols, and share moments of reflection.

- *Decorating the Home:* Danish homes are transformed into havens of warmth and comfort during Christmas. Families take great pride in decorating their homes with candles, twinkling lights, and ornaments. The Christmas tree is the centerpiece, adorned with handmade decorations, and surrounded by wrapped gifts. The scent of pine fills the air, bringing a sense of natural beauty and freshness indoors.

- *Hyggeknas:* Christmas gatherings often include a hyggeknas, which translates to a cozy get-together. Friends and family come together to share a meal, exchange gifts, and enjoy each other's company. The table is set with festive dishes, such as roast duck or pork, caramelized potatoes, and red cabbage. The atmosphere is filled with laughter, storytelling, and heartfelt conversations, creating a sense of togetherness and joy.

- *Danish Christmas Treats:* Danish Christmas treats play a significant role in the holiday celebrations. Families indulge in an array of delicious treats, such as æbleskiver (round pancake puffs), pebernødder (spiced cookies), and klejner (twisted pastries). Baking and sharing these treats is a cherished tradition that brings people together and fills the home with delightful aromas.

- *Candlelit Christmas Eve:* Christmas Eve holds special significance in Denmark. Families gather for a festive meal, usually consisting of a traditional Christmas dinner with roasted meats, potatoes, and various side dishes. As darkness falls, the candles are lit, creating a soft, warm glow throughout the home. The tree is revealed, and the joyous tradition of exchanging gifts begins. Christmas carols are sung, and heartfelt moments of gratitude and love are shared.

The magic of Danish Christmas lies in the emphasis on creating a sense of coziness, love, and togetherness. The traditions evoke feelings of warmth and contentment, allowing people to embrace the spirit of hygge during this special time of year.

New Year's Eve

New Year's Eve, or Nytårsaften, in Denmark is a time for reflection, celebration, and embracing the new beginnings. Many people gather with friends and family for cozy dinner parties, enjoying good food, laughter, and meaningful conversations. As the clock strikes midnight, fireworks light up the sky, and everyone joins in the tradition of toasting with champagne and exchanging well wishes for the year ahead.

Here are some ways in which hygge is woven into the fabric of New Year's Eve traditions:

- <u>*Gathering with Loved Ones:*</u> New Year's Eve is a time for gathering with family and friends to bid farewell to the old year and welcome the new one. People often host intimate parties or attend larger public celebrations. The emphasis is on being surrounded by loved ones, creating a cozy and joyful atmosphere.

- *Hygge Dinner:* A festive dinner is typically prepared for the occasion. It often includes special dishes, such as seafood, roast pork, or a hearty stew. The table is adorned with candles, beautiful table settings, and decorations to create an inviting ambiance.

- *Champagne and Toasts:* As midnight approaches, champagne is poured, and a toast is made to welcome the new year. The clinking of glasses and the shared moment of celebration bring people together in a spirit of joy and anticipation.

- *Fireworks and Bonfires:* Fireworks are an integral part of Danish New Year's Eve celebrations. Families and friends gather outdoors to witness the dazzling displays of light and color. Bonfires are also lit on beaches and in open areas, symbolizing the burning away of the old year and welcoming the new one with warmth and light.

- *New Year's Speech:* The Danish Queen traditionally addresses the nation in a televised New Year's speech. Her words reflect on the past year and offer messages of hope, unity, and gratitude. This speech is an important moment that brings the entire country together and fosters a sense of shared connection and reflection.

- *<u>Midnight Kiss:</u>* It is a common tradition in Denmark for people to exchange a kiss at the stroke of midnight, as a way to welcome the new year and express affection for loved ones. It is a moment filled with warmth and love, symbolizing the importance of human connection and celebrating the future together.

New Year's Eve in Denmark is a time to reflect, celebrate, and embrace the joy of new beginnings. The traditions of the evening, combined with the spirit of hygge, create a cozy and meaningful atmosphere, where people come together to cherish the past year and eagerly embrace the possibilities of the year ahead.

Easter

Easter in Denmark is a time of rebirth and renewal. Families come together to decorate eggs and create intricate paper cutouts known as "gækkebreve" to exchange with loved ones. Traditional Easter lunches feature a variety of delicious dishes, including pickled herring, smoked salmon, and Danish pastries. Outdoor activities such as egg hunting and nature walks are also embraced, allowing people to connect with nature and enjoy the beauty of the changing season.

So, Easter, or Påske, holds special significance in Denmark and is celebrated with hygge traditions and customs. Here are some deeper insights into the hygge practices associated with Easter:

- *Decorating Easter Eggs:* Decorating eggs is a cherished Easter tradition in Denmark. Families gather to dye hard-boiled eggs in vibrant colors, often using natural dyes from onion skins or beetroot. It is a creative and playful activity that brings joy and beauty to the home.

- *Easter Lunch:* Easter Sunday is typically marked by a festive lunch with family and friends. A traditional Danish Easter lunch, known as påskefrokost, is a sumptuous affair featuring an array of delicious dishes, such as pickled herring, smoked salmon, liver pate, and various types of cheese. The table is adorned with flowers and candles, creating a warm and inviting atmosphere.

- *Outdoor Activities:* With the arrival of spring, Easter in Denmark often includes outdoor activities that embrace the hygge connection with nature. Families may go for walks in parks or forests, enjoying the budding flowers and the fresh air. Children participate in Easter egg hunts, searching for hidden chocolate eggs or small gifts, which adds an element of excitement and fun to the celebration.

- *Hyggelig Decorations:* Danish homes are adorned with hyggelig Easter decorations. Branches of budding twigs are collected and displayed in vases, decorated with colorful paper cutouts or small ornaments. These branches symbolize the arrival of spring and new life. Additionally, candles and soft lighting create a cozy ambiance during Easter gatherings.

- *Sweet Treats:* Like many Easter celebrations around the world, Danish Easter is associated with indulging in sweet treats. Traditional pastries, such as hot cross buns (krydderboller) and Danish marzipan-filled chocolates (mølleæg), are enjoyed during the Easter season. These delectable treats add a touch of sweetness and delight to the hyggelig Easter celebrations.

- *Church Services and Reflection:* Easter Sunday holds religious significance, and attending church services is common for many Danes. It is a time for reflection, gratitude, and celebrating the resurrection of Jesus Christ.

Churches are often beautifully decorated with flowers, creating a serene and contemplative atmosphere.

Easter in Denmark is a time of renewal, celebration, and togetherness. By embracing hygge traditions and customs, Danish families create warm and welcoming environments, filled with joy, good food, and meaningful connections. The focus on simplicity, nature, and shared moments makes Easter a special and hyggelig time of year.

Midsummer's Eve

Midsummer Eve, also known as Sankt Hans Aften, is a beloved Danish celebration that takes place on the evening of June 23rd, coinciding with the summer solstice. It is a time of joy and merriment, steeped in hygge traditions. Bonfires are lit on the beach or in parks, and people gather around them to sing songs, share stories, and enjoy the warm summer night. It is a time to celebrate the longest day of the year and embrace the magic of the summer season. Families often enjoy picnics or barbecues, and children engage in games and activities, fostering a sense of community and connection.

Here are some deeper insights into the hygge practices associated with Midsummer Eve:

- *Bonfires:* Lighting bonfires is a central aspect of Midsummer Eve celebrations in Denmark. Communities gather around bonfires on the beach, in parks, or in designated areas to enjoy the warmth and glow of the fire. The bonfires symbolize the triumph of light over darkness and create a cozy and festive ambiance.

- *Outdoor Gatherings:* Midsummer Eve is a time for gathering with family, friends, and neighbors to celebrate the longest day of the year. People come together for picnics, barbecues, and outdoor feasts. It is common to bring blankets, chairs, and picnic baskets filled with delicious food and drinks. Sharing a meal in nature's embrace fosters a sense of togetherness and connection.

- *Music and Dancing:* Traditional music and folk dances are an integral part of Midsummer Eve celebrations. People join in lively circle dances around the bonfire, accompanied by music played on accordions, fiddles, and other instruments. The infectious rhythms and communal dancing create a joyful and festive atmosphere.

- *Flower Crowns:* Midsummer Eve is a time when many people wear flower crowns, especially young girls and women. These crowns are made from fresh flowers and greenery, symbolizing the beauty and abundance of summer. Creating and wearing flower crowns adds a touch of whimsy and natural elegance to the festivities.

- *Storytelling and Legends:* Midsummer Eve is associated with ancient legends and folklore. It is believed that on this night, witches and magical beings are particularly active. People share stories and legends passed down through generations, adding an element of mystery and enchantment to the celebrations.

- *Reflection and Gratitude:* As the sun reaches its peak and the days begin to shorten, Midsummer Eve is a time for reflection and gratitude. It is an opportunity to appreciate the beauty of nature, the warmth of community, and the blessings of the year so far. Taking moments for quiet contemplation and expressing gratitude for the abundance in life is an important aspect of the celebration.

Midsummer Eve in Denmark is a magical and hyggelig celebration that embraces the light and warmth of the summer season. Through bonfires, gatherings, music, and traditions, Danes come together to create a sense of joy, connection, and appreciation for the beauty of nature and community. It is a time to savor the long summer days and create lasting memories with loved ones.

Hygge Fridays

While not associated with a specific holiday, Hygge Fridays are a popular tradition in Denmark. It involves dedicating Fridays as a time to unwind, relax, and enjoy simple pleasures with loved ones. People often gather for cozy dinners, movie nights, or game sessions. The focus is on creating a peaceful atmosphere, free from stress and obligations, and embracing the joy of being present in the moment.

Hygge Fridays, also known as Fredagsmys in Swedish, are a popular tradition that embraces the hygge philosophy and sets the tone for a cozy and relaxing start to the weekend. Here are some deeper insights into the hygge practices associated with Hygge Fridays:

- *Quality Time with Loved Ones:* Hygge Fridays are all about spending quality time with family and close friends. It's an opportunity to unwind, connect, and create lasting memories. Whether it's gathering around the dinner table, enjoying a movie night, or engaging in board games or other activities, the focus is on fostering strong relationships and meaningful connections.

- *Comfortable Attire:* Hygge Fridays call for comfortable and cozy clothing. It's a chance to change into your favorite loungewear, snuggle up in soft blankets, and slip into warm socks or slippers. By embracing comfortable attire, you create a sense of relaxation and ease, allowing yourself to fully unwind and embrace the hygge atmosphere.

- *Delicious Food and Drinks:* Food plays a central role in Hygge Fridays. It's a time to indulge in comforting and delicious meals. Whether it's cooking a homemade dinner, ordering takeout from your favorite restaurant, or preparing a spread of snacks and treats, the focus is on enjoying good food together. Pair your meals with hot beverages like tea, cocoa, or mulled wine to enhance the cozy ambiance.

- _Candlelight and Soft Lighting:_ Hygge Fridays are incomplete without the warm glow of candlelight and soft lighting. Light some candles throughout your home to create a soothing and inviting atmosphere. Dim or soft lighting helps create a sense of relaxation and intimacy, making the space feel cozy and serene.

- _Unplugging and Mindfulness:_ Hygge Fridays provide an opportunity to unplug from technology and be present in the moment. Put away your phones, turn off screens, and engage in activities that promote mindfulness. This could include reading a book, practicing meditation or yoga, journaling, or simply engaging in quiet reflection. Embracing mindfulness allows you to fully appreciate the hygge experience and be in tune with your own well-being.

- _Cozy Entertainment:_ Hygge Fridays offer a chance to enjoy cozy entertainment that promotes relaxation and enjoyment. This could involve watching a movie or TV series, listening to soothing music, playing board games, or engaging in hobbies such as knitting or crafting. The key is to choose activities that bring you joy and allow you to unwind in a cozy environment.

Hygge Fridays are a wonderful way to transition into the weekend and create a hyggelig atmosphere that nourishes your well-being. By prioritizing quality time, comfort, delicious food, and mindfulness, you set the stage for a relaxing and enjoyable evening that helps you recharge and find contentment.

These traditions reflect the essence of hygge, emphasizing togetherness, comfort, and creating a sense of warmth and coziness. By participating in these traditions, individuals not only celebrate specific holidays but also cultivate a deeper connection with loved ones and the joyous moments that life brings.

Chapter 6: Hygge Beyond Denmark: Similar Concepts in Different Cultures

Cozy and Contentment-Focused Concepts in Other Cultures

Across the globe, various cultures have embraced the concept of coziness, contentment, and well-being in their own unique ways. From the Swedish notion of "lagom" to the German concept of "Gemütlichkeit" and the Japanese philosophy of "Wabi-Sabi," these cultural traditions emphasize finding joy in simplicity, creating welcoming spaces, and appreciating life's imperfections. Each philosophy offers its own insights and practices for cultivating comfort, connection, and a sense of belonging. Exploring these cozy and comfort-focused philosophies from different countries not only enriches our understanding of different cultures but also provides inspiration for incorporating elements of coziness and contentment into our own lives. By embracing these concepts, we can create spaces and moments that nurture our well-being and foster a deeper appreciation for the simple pleasures of life.

So, cozy and contentment-focused concepts can be found in various cultures around the world, each with their own unique traditions and practices. Let's explore a few examples:

- *Lagom (Sweden):* Lagom is a Swedish concept that translates to "just the right amount." It promotes a balanced and moderate approach to life, emphasizing simplicity, sustainability, and finding contentment in everyday moments. It encourages a sense of harmony and avoiding extremes.

- *Gemütlichkeit (Germany):* Gemütlichkeit is a German term that embodies a feeling of warmth, comfort, and coziness. It emphasizes creating a welcoming and hospitable atmosphere, often accompanied by good food, close friends, and a sense of togetherness.

- *Wabi-Sabi (Japan):* Wabi-Sabi is a Japanese philosophy that embraces the beauty of imperfection and impermanence. It celebrates the simplicity and naturalness of things, finding beauty in the imperfect, weathered, and aged. It encourages mindfulness, acceptance, and appreciating the present moment.

- *Hyggelig (Norway):* Similar to hygge, hyggelig is a Norwegian concept that focuses on creating a warm and cozy atmosphere. It involves embracing simple pleasures, such as spending time with loved ones, enjoying good food and drinks, and surrounding oneself with comfort and tranquility.

- *Ubuntu (Southern Africa):* Ubuntu is an African philosophy that emphasizes the interconnectedness and shared humanity among people. It promotes compassion, empathy, and the idea that our well-being is tied to the well-being of others. Creating a sense of community and fostering positive relationships are key aspects of ubuntu.

- *Fika (Sweden):* Fika is a Swedish tradition that revolves around taking a break and enjoying a cup of coffee or tea with a sweet treat. It is a cherished moment of relaxation and connection, often shared with friends, family, or colleagues. Fika encourages slowing down, engaging in meaningful conversations, and nurturing relationships.

- *Cwtch (Wales):* Cwtch is a Welsh term that encompasses the feeling of a warm, safe, and cozy embrace. It goes beyond physical touch and embodies a sense of comfort, love, and emotional support. Cwtch encourages creating nurturing spaces and cultivating deep connections with others.

- *Pachamama (Andean cultures):* Pachamama is a concept in Andean cultures that represents Mother Earth and the interconnectedness of all living beings. It emphasizes living in harmony with nature, honoring the earth's resources, and recognizing our role as caretakers of the environment. Connecting with nature and practicing gratitude are central to the Pachamama philosophy.

These are just a few examples of the many cultures that have their own versions of cozy and contentment-focused concepts. Exploring these concepts from different cultures can inspire us to incorporate elements of comfort, simplicity, and mindfulness into our own lives, enhancing our well-being and cultivating a greater sense of joy and contentment.

In the upcoming section, we will delve deeper into the Swedish and Norwegian versions of coziness and contentment, comparing them with the Danish concept of hygge. Despite their similarities, exploring these variations may provide interesting insights and the opportunity to discover elements that resonate with you. It's worth exploring these cultural concepts further to incorporate elements of hygge, "mys," or "kos" into your own life.

Danish "Hygge", Swedish "Mys", or Norwegian "Kos": Difference and Similarities

Beyond the borders of Denmark, other Nordic countries embrace their own versions of coziness and contentment. In Sweden, there's 'mys,' a concept that embodies the warmth and comfort of shared moments with loved ones. Meanwhile, in Norway, 'kos' emphasizes the joy found in simple pleasures and the nurturing of a cozy atmosphere. These cultural concepts share similarities with the Danish concept of hygge, as they all revolve around creating a welcoming and intimate ambiance, fostering meaningful connections, and finding solace in everyday moments. While the specific expressions may vary, they all encapsulate the essence of finding joy, tranquility, and well-being through coziness and mindful living. Let's delve into the nuances of these concepts, exploring their unique cultural contexts and the ways in which they can enrich our lives.

So, "Mys" is a Swedish term and "kos" is a Norwegian term, both of which represent the concept of coziness, comfort, and creating a warm atmosphere. These words are often used to describe the feeling of relaxation, contentment, and enjoying simple pleasures in the company of loved ones.

In Sweden, "mys" encompasses activities such as snuggling up in a blanket, lighting candles, and indulging in delicious food and drinks. It is about creating a cozy environment and taking time to unwind and enjoy the present moment. "Mys" can be experienced individually or shared with friends and family.

Similarly, in Norway, "kos" revolves around creating a warm and inviting atmosphere that promotes relaxation and connection. It involves activities like gathering around a fireplace, savoring hot beverages, and engaging in meaningful conversations. "Kos" emphasizes the importance of slowing down, finding comfort in the little things, and fostering a sense of togetherness.

Both "mys" and "kos" highlight the Scandinavian tradition of embracing coziness and finding joy in simple, everyday moments. These concepts encourage individuals to create welcoming environments, prioritize self-care, and cultivate a sense of well-being and contentment in their lives.

While hygge, "mys," and "kos" share similarities as cozy and comfort-focused concepts, there are also distinct characteristics that set them apart. Here's a comparison and contrast of these concepts:

Origin and Cultural Background

- Hygge: Originates from Denmark and is deeply ingrained in Danish culture and lifestyle.

- "Mys": Swedish term that embodies the Swedish way of life and is a fundamental aspect of Swedish culture.

- "Kos": Norwegian term rooted in Norwegian traditions and customs, reflecting the Norwegian way of creating coziness.

Emphasis on Atmosphere

- Hygge: Focuses on creating a warm and inviting atmosphere, often through the use of candles, soft lighting, and cozy textiles.

- "Mys": Emphasizes a cozy and intimate atmosphere, often achieved through dim lighting, comfortable furnishings, and a relaxed ambiance.

- "Kos": Highlights the importance of a warm and welcoming atmosphere, often involving elements like candles, fireplaces, and comfortable seating.

Social Connection and Togetherness

- Hygge: Values the company of loved ones and emphasizes spending quality time together, fostering deeper connections.

- "Mys": Encourages socializing and bonding with family and friends, often through shared activities, conversations, and meals.

- "Kos": Emphasizes the importance of togetherness, creating a sense of belonging, and enjoying the company of others.

Simplicity and Mindfulness

- Hygge: Celebrates the simplicity of life, finding joy in small pleasures, and being present in the moment.

- "Mys": Encourages mindfulness, appreciating the little things, and embracing a slower pace of life.

- "Kos": Values simplicity, cherishing the ordinary moments, and finding contentment in everyday experiences.

Cultural Expressions

- Hygge: Expressed through cozy gatherings, comfort food, and enjoying indoor activities like reading, knitting, or board games.

- "Mys": Expressed through nature retreats, enjoying outdoor activities, and embracing the beauty of the Swedish countryside.

- "Kos": Expressed through socializing at home or in cafes, enjoying coffee breaks, and embracing nature's beauty.

These concepts celebrate the art of finding joy in life's simple pleasures and creating a sense of warmth and contentment in different ways, reflecting the unique cultural perspectives of Denmark, Sweden, and Norway.

In addition to the comparisons and contrasts mentioned earlier, it's worth noting that hygge, "mys," and "kos" not only create a cozy atmosphere but also encompass a deeper cultural understanding and appreciation of well-being. They reflect the values and priorities of their respective cultures, emphasizing the importance of finding balance, nurturing relationships, and finding comfort in everyday moments.

These concepts go beyond mere physical comfort and delve into the emotional and psychological aspects of well-being. They encourage individuals to prioritize self-care, relaxation, and meaningful connections with loved ones. Whether it's curling up with a book by the fireplace, enjoying a home-cooked meal with friends, or taking a peaceful walk in nature, these practices remind us to slow down, savor the present, and find contentment in the simple pleasures of life.

While each concept has its unique cultural context, they all share a common goal: promoting a sense of happiness, relaxation, and fulfillment. By embracing these philosophies, individuals can enhance their well-being, strengthen their relationships, and cultivate a greater appreciation for the beauty and joy that can be found in everyday experiences.

As the universal human desire for well-being, comfort, and a sense of belonging lies at the heart of all these philosophies, it is likely that you, too, have been drawn to this book in search of happiness, joy, and contentment. In this final part, I would like to take a moment to reflect on this essential matter and share a few thoughts.

Universal Human Desires: Comfort, Well-Being, and a Sense of Belonging

Universal human desires for comfort, well-being, and a sense of belonging are fundamental aspects of our existence. Regardless of cultural or geographical differences, these desires are shared by people around the world.

Comfort is a basic human need that encompasses physical, emotional, and psychological well-being. We seek comfort to feel safe, relaxed, and at ease. It involves creating an environment that nurtures our senses and allows us to recharge and replenish our energy. Whether it's finding warmth in a cozy blanket, enjoying a comforting meal, or surrounding ourselves with familiar and soothing elements, the pursuit of comfort is deeply ingrained in our nature.

Well-being is another universal desire, as it encompasses our overall state of health and happiness. We strive for a sense of well-being in various aspects of our lives, including our physical, mental, and emotional states. It involves taking care of ourselves, maintaining balance, and finding fulfillment. Cultivating well-being means nourishing our bodies, engaging in activities that bring us joy and fulfillment, and cultivating positive relationships and connections with others.

A sense of belonging is also inherent to human nature. We have an innate need to feel connected, accepted, and understood by others. We seek to be part of communities, families, and social networks that provide us with a sense of belonging and identity. This connection and belongingness contribute to our overall well-being and play a significant role in our happiness and fulfillment.

Hygge, along with other cultural concepts, recognizes and addresses these universal human desires. By embracing the principles of comfort, well-being, and belonging, we can create environments and lifestyles that prioritize our overall happiness and contentment. Regardless of cultural backgrounds or geographical locations, these desires remain constant, and our pursuit of them unites us in our shared human experience.

In addition to the universal human desires for comfort, well-being, and a sense of belonging, it's important to recognize that these desires are interconnected and mutually reinforcing. When we experience comfort, it contributes to our well-being by reducing stress, promoting relaxation, and enhancing our overall mood. Similarly, when we prioritize our well-being through self-care practices and positive lifestyle choices, it enhances our sense of comfort and contentment. Furthermore, a sense of belonging and social connection plays a significant role in our well-being, as it provides emotional support, a sense of identity, and a network of relationships that contribute to our overall happiness.

Cultivating hygge, along with similar concepts, acknowledges the holistic nature of these desires and offers a framework for integrating them into our lives. By nurturing comfort, well-being, and a sense of belonging, we create an environment that fosters happiness, fulfillment, and a deep connection to ourselves and others. It is through this recognition and intentional cultivation that we can enhance our overall quality of life and find greater joy in the simple pleasures of everyday existence.

Conclusion

Embrace Hygge in Your Life

Throughout this book, we have explored the essence of hygge and its transformative power in enhancing our well-being and overall quality of life. We have delved into the core principles of hygge, such as coziness, togetherness, mindfulness, and simplicity, understanding how they create a harmonious and fulfilling existence. We have learned to create cozy and inviting spaces, foster meaningful connections, prioritize self-care, and embrace the beauty of the present moment.

The key takeaway is that hygge offers us a profound invitation to slow down, savor the simple joys, and cultivate a sense of comfort, contentment, and belonging in our lives. It reminds us to find happiness in the little things, to cherish moments of togetherness, and to prioritize our well-being. By incorporating hygge into our daily lives, we can create an environment that nourishes our souls, reduces stress, and brings us closer to the people and experiences that truly matter.

As we reach the conclusion of this journey, I encourage you, dear reader, to embrace hygge as a way of life. Take the principles and practices you have discovered within these pages and infuse them into your daily routines, interactions, and surroundings. Let hygge be your guide in creating a sanctuary of comfort, a haven of joy, and a refuge from the hustle and bustle of modern life.

Remember, hygge is not just a fleeting trend or a passing fad—it is a timeless philosophy that speaks to our deepest human needs for connection, happiness, and a life well-lived. So, light those candles, gather with loved ones, savor the flavors, and immerse yourself in the cozy embrace of hygge. May it bring you warmth, peace, and a renewed appreciation for the beauty that surrounds you.

Embrace hygge, and may it become a cherished companion on your journey towards a more fulfilling and joyful existence.

Dear reader, it's important to remember that incorporating hygge is a personal journey that can be tailored to your own preferences and needs. Your interpretation and practice of hygge may differ from others, and that's perfectly okay. The essence of hygge lies in creating an environment and lifestyle that brings you comfort and happiness, so trust your instincts and follow what resonates with you.

Not only does hygge benefit your individual well-being, but it also has the power to strengthen your relationships and deepen your connections with loved ones. I encourage you to share the joy of hygge with those around you. Invite them to join you in creating cozy moments and building cherished memories together. By embracing hygge collectively, you can foster a sense of community and support that enriches everyone's lives.

It's worth noting that hygge is not limited to specific seasons or occasions. While it's often associated with cozy winter nights, the spirit of hygge can be experienced all year round. Whether you're enjoying outdoor activities in the summer, creating a cozy reading nook in the spring, or relishing in the beauty of autumn, hygge can be woven into every season. It's a mindset that allows you to find comfort and contentment in all moments, no matter the time of year.

By keeping these points in mind, you'll have a comprehensive understanding of hygge and be motivated to incorporate its principles and practices into your daily life. Embracing hygge will not only enhance your well-being but also cultivate deeper connections and a greater sense of joy and fulfillment. So go forth, dear reader, and create your own hygge-filled world.

Wishing you warmth, happiness, and countless cozy moments.

Prioritize Coziness, Mindfulness, and Togetherness for Overall Well-Being

As we come to the conclusion of this book, I want to reinforce the importance of prioritizing coziness, mindfulness, and togetherness for your overall well-being. In our busy and often stressful lives, we often overlook the simple pleasures that bring us joy and nourish our souls. By intentionally embracing the principles of hygge, we create space for coziness, allowing ourselves to unwind, relax, and recharge. This deliberate focus on creating a cozy environment cultivates a sense of comfort and security, providing a sanctuary from the demands of the outside world.

Mindfulness is another essential aspect of well-being. By being present in the moment and savoring the small joys of everyday life, we develop a deeper appreciation for the beauty and simplicity that surrounds us. I encourage you to engage in mindful practices such as meditation, deep breathing, or mindful walks to foster a sense of inner calm and clarity.

But perhaps one of the most transformative aspects of embracing hygge is the power of togetherness. Human connection and meaningful relationships are fundamental to our happiness. I urge you to prioritize quality time with loved ones, creating opportunities for shared experiences, heartfelt conversations, and genuine connections. Nurture your relationships and build a strong support system, as these bonds provide a sense of belonging, acceptance, and support.

By prioritizing coziness, mindfulness, and togetherness, you empower yourself to make conscious choices that contribute to your overall well-being. Embracing the hygge lifestyle is a journey that requires intention, practice, and self-compassion. Discover the transformative power that hygge can have on your physical, emotional, and mental well-being.

In addition to enhancing your personal well-being, embracing hygge can have a lasting impact on various aspects of your life. By reducing stress, fostering contentment, and promoting self-care, hygge improves your mental and emotional well-being. Creating hygge-inspired environments and engaging in shared hygge activities deepen your connections with loved ones, strengthen your support system, and cultivate a sense of belonging. Spread the hygge philosophy by sharing your experiences, inviting others to join in hygge activities, and creating welcoming spaces for all.

Remember, hygge is not limited to individual practices or specific moments. It is a mindset—a way of approaching life with warmth, intention, and an appreciation for the present moment. Embrace the power of hygge and experience the profound benefits it can bring to your life and the lives of those around you.

Farewell...

Dear reader,

As we come to the end of our journey exploring the world of hygge, I want to leave you with a heartfelt hyggish salute and a wish for happiness, well-being, and all the good things that come with embracing hygge in your lives.

May your days be filled with cozy moments that warm your heart and soothe your soul. May you find comfort in the simple pleasures of life, whether it's curling up with a good book, sipping a warm cup of tea, or enjoying the company of loved ones. May you cultivate mindfulness and be fully present in each precious moment, finding joy in the beauty that surrounds you.

May your relationships be nourished by the spirit of togetherness and deep connections. May you create spaces that invite laughter, meaningful conversations, and a sense of belonging. May your shared experiences with family and friends be filled with love, laughter, and cherished memories that last a lifetime.

And as you embrace the hygge philosophy, may it extend beyond your personal sphere and touch the lives of those around you. May your kindness and empathy create ripples of positivity in your communities, fostering a sense of unity and support. May you be a beacon of hygge, inviting others to join in the pursuit of comfort, well-being, and a more joyful way of living.

Remember, hygge is not just a fleeting trend or a concept to be understood intellectually. It is a way of being, a way of embracing life with open arms and an open heart. It is about finding beauty and happiness in the ordinary, and savoring the small moments that often go unnoticed. So, my dear readers, may you continue to invite hygge into your lives and let it be a guiding light on your journey to a more fulfilling and contented existence.

With warm wishes and a hyggish salute,

Freja